WITHDRAWN

Women in Print
II

Opportunities for Women's Studies
Publication in Language
and Literature

Edited by
Joan E. Hartman
and
Ellen Messer-Davidow

for the Commission on
the Status of Women in the Profession

THE MODERN LANGUAGE ASSOCIATION
OF AMERICA
NEW YORK 1982

Copyright © 1982 by The Modern Language Association of America

Library of Congress Cataloging in Publication Data (Revised)

Main entry under title:

Women in print.

Includes bibliographical references.

Contents: 1. Opportunities for women's studies research in language and literature. 2. Opportunities for women's studies publication in language and literature.

1. Women and literature—Addresses, essays, lectures. I. Hartman, Joan. II. Messer-Davidow, Ellen, 1941-   . III. Modern Language Association of America. Commission on the Status of Women in the Profession.

PN481.W656   809'.89287   82-3596

ISBN 0-87352-336-9 (v. 1)

ISBN 0-87352-337-7 (pbk. : v. 1)

ISBN 0-87352-338-5 (v. 2)

ISBN 0-87352-339-3 (pbk. : v. 2)

PN
481.
W656
1982
v. 2

Published by The Modern Language Association of America
62 Fifth Avenue, New York, New York 10011

Contents

Introduction
Joan E. Hartman and Ellen Messer-Davidow   1

Establishment Publishing

Feminist Scholarship and the University Press
Carol Orr   13

Publishing Opportunities Abroad (Particularly in France)
Jean A. Perkins   23

Scholarly Reprint Publishing
Ralph Carlson   29

Textbook Publishing: Some Notes on Responsibility
Ronald Mallis   35

Boards and Paper: Feminist Writing and Trade Publishing
Martha M. Kinney   41

Academic Writing and Rejection
Emily Toth   57

What's in a Name? The Case for Author-Anonymous
Reviewing Policies
Domna C. Stanton   65

Making Choices: Can Two Small-Town Feminists Publish
with a Big-City Trade House and Remain Pure?
Susan Griffin and J. J. Wilson   79

Alternative Publishing

Feminist Presses
Shirley Frank   89

Feminist Texts and the Nonestablishment Press
Angelika Bammer   117

Feminist Journals: Writing for a Feminist Future
Charlotte Bunch   139

Other Words: Alternative Publishing Outlets for Women Writers
Ann Romines and Thomazine W. Shanahan   153

Notes on Contributors   171

Introduction

Women in Print, the title of these two volumes sponsored by the Modern Language Association Commission on the Status of Women in the Profession, refers to the women authors who are—or should be—the subjects of our research, publication, and teaching and to ourselves as publishing scholars, critics, and teachers of women's studies in language and literature. *Women in Print I: Opportunities for Women's Studies Research in Language and Literature* assesses areas where research and publication are needed—in the fundamental tasks of scholarship, in the study of language, in the national literatures, and in the literature produced by women writers who have been neglected on grounds of class, race, and sociosexual orientation. *Women in Print II: Opportunities for Women's Studies Publication in Language and Literature* surveys ways and means to further the publication of women's studies in language and literature; it explores the nature, requirements, and resources of both establishment and alternative publishing.

When the MLA Commission on the Status of Women was established in 1969, courses in women's studies were beginning to be taught in colleges and universities throughout the United States, and then, as now, courses in literature figured prominently among them. By 1976 there were 270 women's studies programs and an estimated 15,000 courses offered at some 1,500 different institutions (Florence Howe, *Seven Years Later: Women's Studies Programs in 1976* [n.p.: National

1

Advisory Council on Women's Studies Programs, 1977], p. 15). Between one third and one half of these courses were offered in the humanities, and of these, half—or, at a conservative estimate, 2,500 courses—were offered in literature. By 1981 the number of women's studies programs had risen from 270 to 328 (*PMLA*, 96 [1981], 716–21) and by December 1981 there were 2,316 members of the MLA Division of Women's Studies in Language and Literature, making it the sixth largest division in MLA. The women who teach and study language and literature have contributed substantially to the development of women's studies and are substantially investing their professional energy and status in this field.

The members of the MLA Commission on the Status of Women are mindful that the charge to monitor and improve the status of women in the profession requires an advocacy not only of women as scholars, teachers, and students but also of women's literary productions and lives as subjects meriting serious and sustained inquiry. We recognize too that the work of augmenting and dispersing knowledge about women writers, of challenging their exclusion from the literary canon and the classroom, and of seeing that suitable texts are available for teaching and research can afford women opportunities for publication and for enhancing their professional reputations. That some scholars in the modern languages are doing research and writing about women authors we know from the papers they present—at national and regional MLA meetings and at women's studies conferences—as well as from what they publish: they are recording female literary history, creating feminist pedagogy, and devising feminist critiques of literature, criticism, and language. But are enough women aware of the possibilities for women's studies research, and are there sufficient opportunities for them to publish?

The commission's "Study III: Women in Modern Language Departments, 1972–73" (*PMLA*, 91 [1976], 124–36) shows, not surprisingly, that publication is a major predictor of rank, tenure, and salary in English and foreign language departments. Women do not publish as much as men, perhaps partly because of a disparity in status. A smaller percentage of women teachers than of men teachers hold Ph.D.'s, and a larger percentage of women than of men are in the lower ranks at all institutions and in all ranks at institutions where teaching loads are high. Consequently women do more than their share of the profession's teaching. But, even taking into account these imbalances, the commission felt that women could do a larger share of the profession's publishing. It suggested that publishers and editors might be less receptive to manuscripts by women than to those by men, that they might be inadequately informed about the value of and need for women's studies materials, and that, in turn, women's studies scholars might require a fuller understanding of the publishing industry.

In response to these considerations, the commission identified publishing as a promising area in which to begin working for change. Toward that end, the members planned a conference for 2 April 1976 in New York, inviting representatives from university presses, commercial publishers, and periodicals to attend a day of workshops on bibliography, scholarship, reprints, texts, anthologies and popular writings, and periodicals. Conducted jointly by editors and by women's studies scholars and teachers, the workshops aimed at an exchange of information. On the one hand, the commission wished to learn about the editors' processes of submission, review, and contracting; their economic and marketing policies; their selection of manuscript readers; their criteria for judging manuscripts; their interest in women's studies in language and literature; and any constraints they felt about publishing women's studies materials. On the other, the commission also wished to let the editors know about the identity and size of the potential market for women's studies publications, the value of women's studies as a field of inquiry and teaching, the nature and amount of research under way, and the work that remained to be done and to be published.

Encouraged by the publishers' receptiveness and eager to disperse the findings of the conference to women's studies scholars and teachers, Joan E. Hartman and Ellen Messer-Davidow, the editors of this two-volume work, arranged several workshops: one, Women in Print, in December 1976 at the MLA meeting in San Francisco; another in June 1979 at the National Women's Studies Association conference in Lawrence, Kansas; and a third in November 1979 at the American Educational Research Association conference in Cleveland, Ohio. Meanwhile, we were planning this publication to enlarge on matters discussed at the April 1976 conference and to reach a wider audience than we could through conferences. In soliciting contributions, we emphasized the provisional nature of *Women in Print:* the two volumes inquire into possible directions for research, make a preliminary survey of the available resources, and provide a tentative guide to our needs in research and publication.

Women in Print II: Opportunities for Women's Studies Publication in Language and Literature is a how-to volume: how and where to get into print. If *Women in Print I* derives from talks on feminist research given by the scholars who spoke at the commission's April 1976 conference in New York, this volume elaborates what the editors had to say about the nature, resources, and requirements of their various publishing enterprises. Four essays in the first section, Establishment Publishing, are written by editors who spoke at the conference. Carol Orr, then assistant director of the Princeton University Press and now director of the University of Tennessee Press, discussed university press publishing. Ralph Carlson, senior editor of Garland Publishing, discussed scholarly reprint publishing. Martha M. Kinney, then with Dell and now senior editor of Viking-Penguin, talked about trade and mass-market paperback publishing. Ronald Mallis, then English editor at Houghton Mifflin, spoke on textbook publishing. In addition to information about various kinds of publishing, their essays respond to the concerns voiced by the women's studies scholars and teachers who attended the conference.

The section on establishment publishing also contains four essays written by academics with scholarly and editorial experience who take up some of the problems that confront us as scholars, women, and feminists. Jean A. Perkins, professor of French, former cochair of the MLA Commission on the Status of Women, and former president of MLA, writes on scholarly publishing in France and elsewhere abroad. Emily Toth, editor of the now-defunct journal *Regionalism and the Female Imagination*, gives advice on how to avoid manuscript rejection in writing scholarly articles and dealing with journal editors. Domna C. Stanton, former cochair of the MLA Commission on the Status of Women and former associate editor of *Signs: Journal of Women in Culture and Society*, discusses the importance of author-anonymous reviewing (that is, reviewing manuscripts whose authors are not identified) to academic women. Susan Griffin, poet and essayist, and J. J. Wilson, teacher and scholar, together consider the advantages and disadvantages of publishing with a trade house rather than with a feminist press.

The second section of *Women in Print II* contains four essays that explore alternative publishing outlets and issues. The first two essays, by Shirley Frank and by Angelika Bammer, survey feminist and nonestablishment presses, while the next two essays, by Charlotte Bunch and by Ann Romines and Thomazine W. Shanahan, survey feminist journals and other journals, magazines, and newsletters. Frank, Bammer, and Bunch sent out questionnaires to a selected list of presses and journals, and their essays provide a useful compendium of information about the interests, processes, finances, and readerships of the presses and journals that responded. Romines and Shanahan gathered similar information on periodical publications that, because they are not the standard literary and feminist journals, can be additional outlets for feminist scholarship and writing. The authors of these essays also have diverse professional experience. Shirley Frank is associated with the Feminist Press as managing editor of the *Women's Studies Quarterly* (formerly the *Women's Studies Newsletter*), the official publication of the National Women's Studies Association. Angelika Bammer is the former editor of *Concerns*, the newsletter of the Women's Caucus for the Modern Languages. Charlotte Bunch, an activist and researcher, is an editor of *Quest: A Feminist Quarterly.* Ann Romines does university teaching and Thomazine Shanahan free-lance writing.

Publishing with establishment presses and journals is the way that academic women get the credit they need for tenure and promotion; in addition, it is usually the appropriate mode for the writing we do, scholarship and criticism in women's studies in language and literature. The university press, Carol Orr argues, is best suited to works of scholarship, even when they are of more-than-usual general interest. The advantages of publishing with a university press that she cites are careful editing, excellent design and production, strategic promotion, and long life in print (see also the collection of essays by university press editors, *Scholars and Their Publishers,* ed. Weldon A. Kefauver [New York: MLA, 1977]). Jean A. Perkins, after surveying the limited opportunities to publish in French with French publishers, both academic and trade, concurs with Orr, even though publishing with an American university press mandates writing in English. Ralph Carlson explains the economics and mechanics of a specialized area of publishing, the scholarly reprint series that we need for research, since so many women's writings are available only in a few great research libraries. Taking a lively view of the mixed state of commercial publishing, Martha Kinney describes a decade of impressive trade publishing of feminist books and warns of the conglomeritis and "sweet savage schlock" that are crowding out literary writings (for a more extensive account of trade publishing and its discontents, see Thomas Whiteside's three-part *New Yorker* article [20 Sept.–13 Oct. 1980], reprinted as *The Blockbuster Complex* [Middletown: Wesleyan Univ. Press, 1981]). Ronald Mallis discusses what he calls the "ecology" of textbook publishing and reminds us that content is determined not by publishers but by authors and users—us. To alter content we must educate our colleagues; when we do, he assures us, textbook publishers will respond.

All five of these essays on establishment publishing offer nuts-and-bolts advice about identifying appropriate publishers and proposing and submitting manuscripts. They also delineate the economic constraints and marketing procedures of various kinds of publishing. In addition to imagining the appropriate readers of our works and writing for them, we should count them; when we submit a manuscript our chance of acceptance is greater if we can estimate the number of our readers and the likelihood of their buying what we write. Because women's studies is a new field, we need to educate publishers about its dimensions and also its solidity (nowadays, at least, fewer sales representatives tell us that it's a fad). Our chance of acceptance is also greater when we make felicitous matches between manuscripts and publishers. Martha Kinney neatly differentiates hardcover books, trade paperbacks, and mass-market paperbacks. The books that disappear as we get ready to teach them are usually mass-market paperbacks. Produced for large audiences, they are permitted to go out of print when sales fall and may even be shredded. Trade paperbacks, by contrast, aim at smaller audiences and stay in print longer. Their publishers, Kinney assures us, will keep them in print if we can show the possibility of steady but modest sales. We should not look to scholarly reprint publishers to supply our students with books. Libraries, Ralph Carlson explains, are the chief customers of scholarly reprint houses; although reprint publishers are satisfied with modest sales, they must price their hardcover volumes high to make publishing them pay.

Because university press publication is subsidized, sales are less important than they are in trade publication. But when we submit our manuscripts to a university press we may encounter the response to feminist scholarship and criticism that we also encounter in our institutions: are feminists sufficiently dispassionate? The audience at the commission's 1976 conference was disturbed to hear Carol Orr, herself a supporter of feminist publication, ask this question. In her essay she acknowledges that perhaps, as a woman, she looks for an excellence in feminist scholarship that she would not look for in—in what? In other scholarship, or in masculinist scholarship? Much other scholarship is masculinist scholarship, feminists say, and its dispassion—its lack of passion—comes from its assured hegemony; as a result, our task of pressing for the correction of its single-sex view is only too likely to be called passionate and polemic. Paradoxically, then, feminist writing may fare better with trade publishers, who seek a feminist readership outside the academy, than with university presses, who may not recognize the feminist readership within the academy.

While feminist scholarship and criticism may be rejected for their ideology, they may also be rejected for slightness of intellectual content, poor writing, and ineptness of presentation—and by feminist editors. What "sells" in graduate school, Emily Toth observes, does not "sell" in scholarly journals: graduate school writing lacks authority and an individual voice, both of which may be hard for women to come by. She recommends that in submitting their work scholars choose publications carefully; the new *MLA Directory of Periodicals: A Guide to Journals and Series in Languages and Literatures, 1978–79* (comp. Eileen M. Mackesy, Karen Mateyak, and Diane Siegel [New York: MLA, 1979]), to be updated every two years, will facilitate selection. The *Directory* describes some three thousand journals and series and provides indexes to editorial personnel, languages published, sponsoring organizations, and subjects. There are two references under the subject heading *women* and six more under its five subheadings. The compilers of the *Directory* did not ask journals about their policy with respect to author-anonymous reviewing, a policy instituted for *PMLA* in January 1980. Domna Stanton reviews the debate over this policy as it occurred in the Modern Language Association and amasses evidence that suggests how a female author's name, apart from the feminist content of her article, is the repository of sexual stereotypes that depreciate the value of her words.

The last essay in the section on establishment publishing has the subtitle "Can Two Small-Town Feminists Publish with a Big-City Trade House and Remain Pure?" Its authors, Susan Griffin and J. J. Wilson, have published with Harper and Row as well as with feminist presses. Among the advantages they cite of publishing with a trade house are advances, royalties, distribution, purchase by libraries, and the cachet that wins speaking engagements and grants. These advantages seldom exist in alternative publishing: the responses of feminist and nonestablishment presses to the questionnaires that were sent by our authors reiterate the financial constraints that affect advances, royalties, promotion, and distribution. The more insidious advantages of publishing with a trade house are validation, "recognition by the father," and "permission to take women's writing seriously." Griffin and Wilson are conscious of the interplay between trade and feminist publishers; of the importance, to feminists and to the community, of keeping women's presses alive; and of the need of women writers to organize in order to balance the power of trade publishers. They also cite, as a major factor in their pleasure at publishing with a big-city trade house, working with a feminist editor.

Griffin, who writes poetry and prose, can genuinely choose between establishment and alternative publishing. Wilson, an academic, has fewer opportunities to choose. Scholarship and criticism, as Shirley Frank's article shows, are not well served by feminist presses. Only one press of those she surveyed, Eden Press (Canada), publishes scholarship and criticism, and only three—the Feminist Press (United States), Virago Press (Great Britain), and the Women's Press (Great Britain)—publish reprints with introductions and notes. The others publish creative work, a few publish nonsexist children's books. Feminist scholarship and criticism are not more frequently produced, though for different reasons, by nonestablishment presses. Angelika Bammer, in her essay, divides the forty-six nonestablishment presses that responded to her questionnaire into three groups: artist presses (which publish creative writings), activist presses (all left-oriented), and scholarly presses. The apparent ambivalence of the seventeen artist presses toward feminist writing indicates the real need for feminist presses to get women's creative work into print. The eleven activist presses appear receptive to publishing feminist theory but not women's studies scholarship and criticism. Another seventeen are scholarly presses, one third geared to general readers and the rest to specialized academic audiences. Most appear to support women's studies scholarship and criticism without being willing to publish it, because of their specialized interests. Bammer nevertheless thinks it important that we use the resources of the nonestablishment presses to reach out beyond specialized feminist and academic audiences. For even while we are making our way in the professional realm, it is in our interest as feminists to encourage changes of consciousness and society by learning to "speak our ideas in the common language."

In her essay on feminist journals Charlotte Bunch reports on the editorial policies and practices of the nationally distributed journals she chose to survey. She divides them into three groups according to their primary emphasis: women's studies and academic journals, general feminist movement journals, and literary and art journals. Those in the first group are the journals we created for our scholarship and criticism, the journals in which we first demonstrated not simply the academic legitimacy but also the value of our work. Two of them have survived the stern ranking eye of Michael West; in his review essay "Evaluating Periodicals in English Studies: Tell It in *Gath* if Ye Must, Young Men, but Publish It Not in *Askelon*" (*College English,* 41 [1980], 903–23), he looks at both the *MLA Directory of Periodicals* and *Scholarly Communication: The Report of the National Enquiry* (Baltimore: Johns Hopkins Univ. Press, 1979) and reflects on the state and quality of scholarly journals in English. His title does not cheer a feminist, but he puts *Signs* in his Group B (between *Shakespeare Survey* and *Southern Literary Journal*) and *Women's Studies* (with a plus) in his Group C (between *Western American Literature* and *Wordsworth Circle*). His ranking of English journals should come as no surprise, for we know the academy is intensely hierarchical. Therefore it is important to demonstrate the value—the rank—of feminist scholarship and criticism. But Ann Romines and Thomazine Shanahan agree with Angelika Bammer that we must continue to use the common language, "not so much to lower our sights as to broaden them." Their essay, "Other Words," abounds in suggestions for locating journals, magazines, and newsletters other than the scholarly literary and women's studies periodicals and using them to spread the word. If such publication does not give us credentials in the masculinist academy, it nevertheless keeps us functioning as writers and engages us in the important feminist work of maintaining communication with women outside the academy.

Academic feminists live in multiple worlds, and we hope that *Women in Print II* will help us publish in all of them. Doing so, we join the line of women who published, against hazards, both conventionally and unconventionally, and avoid the fate of that uncertain line whose words are not known. Getting them and ourselves into print is the work of redemption as well as of credentialing.

Joan E. Hartman and Ellen Messer-Davidow
College of Staten Island, City University of New York
University of Cincinnati

Establishment Publishing

Feminist Scholarship and the University Press

Carol Orr

I once received—and returned forthwith—a manuscript that began, "Once upon a time when I was naive, and yes, young, although the two aren't necessarily one, I held the view that one of the first obligations incumbent upon a writer of serious intent was the necessity that he define his terms." Although I am neither young nor naive (nor male), I hold that view. My terms, then, are these: I speak for university presses in general only so far as my own press is representative of university presses in general; my views about feminist scholarship and trade publishers are my own. My definitions are two simple ones: that university presses are publishers of scholarship and that feminist scholarship is first and foremost scholarship, with the adjective " feminist" describing a particular approach to the material at hand. In what follows I intend to provide some practical suggestions to authors who are looking for publishers for their scholarship[1] and to offer a few comments about the state of feminist scholarship from one publisher's point of view.

Selecting and/or Finding the Right Publisher

Assuming an author has a book manuscript and wants to find a publisher, what's the best way to proceed? Two don'ts: first, don't mail the manuscript to just any publisher, and second, don't mail the manu-

13

script at all. If you do, the package is likely to be buried under a huge pile of manuscripts in an editor's office to await its turn. In several weeks, when the manuscript emerges at the top of the pile, the editor may see at a cursory glance that for any number of reasons it is inappropriate for the press. Thus the author has wasted postage and time when the manuscript could have been with the right publisher undergoing a thorough reading.

Instead of shipping off the manuscript, visit a library or a bookstore to get a sense of which publishers specialize in works in your field, which presses publish authors you respect, which presses produce books that appeal to you aesthetically by their design and bookmaking materials.[2] Make a list of appropriate publishers, then compose a letter of inquiry to send to all of them simultaneously.

Address your letter to "Editor" and tell us what we need to know to decide whether we want to see the manuscript. Besides giving the title and number of pages, describe the manuscript in a paragraph or two: its subject, the time period and authors it covers, the methodology it uses, the argument it makes. Suggest why the book should be published, who needs to read it, what contribution it makes. Enclose a table of contents and the introduction if it's short. Ask questions, too. For example, "If you are interested in considering this manuscript and if I submit it to you, when may I expect to receive your reaction to it?" If you use a letter of inquiry, you will almost certainly receive several expressions of interest.

Once you've gathered several expressions of interest, select one publisher to whom to send your manuscript. Multiple submissions are the bane of a press's existence, and for good reason. It costs a publisher a good deal of money to process a manuscript. Adding up the editor's time—which is the press's money—the clerical expenses, general overhead, and readers' fees, processing one manuscript from submission to acceptance costs a press at least $1,000. University presses are marginal operations at best, and they're lucky to break even. Most of them survive through subsidies. They can't afford to use their limited resources to evaluate a manuscript only to discover that the author has decided to sign a contract with another publisher who has also been considering the manuscript. There are, of course, exceptions—cases where an author is justified in asking publishers to compete. But unless publishers have been offering you advances, immense royalties, and finished books in five months, or unless you have written a definitive treatise proving, say, that Margaret Fuller and Henry Thoreau were one and the same androgyne, please submit your manuscript to one publisher at a time.

Advance Contracts

The subject of publishing agreements has been dealt with adequately elsewhere.[3] I would, however, like to say a word about advance contracts.

Although university presses are reputed to be the last bastions of conservative editorial practices, I have recently noticed that some of them have begun to hand out, rather liberally and perhaps injudiciously, advance contracts. These contracts are frequently based on no more than a prospectus, an outline, or the author's description of a project prepared as part of a research-grant application. The author should beware. Such advance contracts might more accurately be called "promises to consider seriously"; they are by no means guarantees to publish. How could they be? There is as yet no manuscript for the press to evaluate. Read the contract carefully. Somewhere there is a clause indicating that the decision to publish is contingent on final approval of the completed manuscript.

If an advance contract is not binding, what are its advantages and disadvantages? If you are a published author with a successful book or books behind you and another book in mind or if you are an unpublished author with an idea for a seminal book, the publisher wants first option and in return promises you that the completed manuscript will receive full attention. The advantage here is primarily the publisher's. But there may be advantages to you as well. You may feel a sense of security in having, even tenuously, a publisher; you can get on with your work, knowing there is someone there to welcome it when it's completed. If you are engaged in a particularly complex project (perhaps editing a symposium), the publisher's advice and guidance can be helpful.[4] You may receive a small advance against royalties, although this practice is rare. And if you are up for review for promotion or tenure, you can inform your department head of the advance contract, although department heads should know that an advance contract does not guarantee eventual publication: at the most it implies that qualified referees have commented favorably on the book proposal; at the least it signifies that the press has exercised a modicum of judgment in recognizing a promising project. The proof of the project is in its successful completion, and many an advance contract collapses, leaving a bitter misunderstanding among press, author, and department. If an advance against royalties is involved, the aftertaste is more bitter.

The passage of time can change even the best advance contract to an author's disadvantage. By the time the manuscript is complete, the editor who sponsored the contract may have left the press and the new editor may not view the project with the same enthusiasm. Or the press may be shifting the focus of its list or experiencing financial constraints and cutting back.

Thus, although one can see the advantages of an advance contract to the publisher, the advantages to the author are ambiguous at best. Why tie yourself down to one publisher so early in the development of a book? If the final manuscript is good, you'll have no trouble finding a publisher; if it's not so good, an advance contract will not get it published. Don't be seduced by the flattery of a paper promise. Don't limit your options.

A Note on Dissertations

Tennessee is now publishing about thirty new books a year, but we are receiving almost three hundred manuscripts. Although the numbers may vary, all university presses are experiencing similar pressures. The competition is keen, particularly among manuscripts in literary criticism. With such an influx of manuscripts, presses haven't the staff and time to read Ph.D. dissertations and offer authors suggestions for revision; we wish we did. A thesis is rarely synonymous with a book manuscript. If the author believes that her dissertation contributes to knowledge, it is her responsibility to revise the work before submitting it to a publisher. Even if the work should require further revision after it has been read by an editor and/or an outside reader, the chances of the manuscript's being read in the first place greatly increase if the author has taken the initiative and the time and trouble to transform the thesis into a book.[5] Sometimes, when the dissertation trappings have been shed, the original contributions may be extracted and published more effectively as journal articles.

University Press or Trade Publisher?

But what if you are that exceptional scholar besieged by both university and trade presses? Which way do you go? First, ask yourself for whom you've written the book. If you are a feminist scholar addressing primarily colleagues in your field (female and male) and academics in related disciplines, then your book by definition calls for the imprint of a university press. But what if your book, while basically a work of scholarship, was written with a broader readership in mind, the so-called general reader or educated layperson? Would a trade publisher do a better job for you than a university press would? Not necessarily. In my opinion, most scholarly books with wider general interest fare better with a university press—for three reasons.

Editorial Input
A book that is intended as a contribution to knowledge needs the rigorous and objective scrutiny it will receive from the university press

editor and the press's scholarly readers.[6] This stringent review process can reveal overlooked sources, weaknesses in an argument, and errors of fact. Tough criticism has transformed many a mediocre manuscript into a good one, many a good manuscript into an excellent book. Remedying faults before publication obviates their being pounced on in book reviews after publication. While some trade publishers do engage professional referees to advise them on nonfiction, I think it is fair to say that their impetus to publish a book is roused less by its scholarly merits than by its sales potential, about which, as I mention later, they are oddly enough often wrong. The desire for excellence that marks a university press's scrutiny of a manuscript before acceptance extends to the copy editing after acceptance. Expert care goes into the copy editing of a university press book and, concomitantly, into its design and production.

Design and Production

Book designers, like scholars, are trained professionals in their field. While the designer will respect an author's color preferences and welcome suggestions for jacket illustrations, the design and manufacture of a book are ultimately the designer's, and thus the publisher's, prerogative and responsibility. If you care about the appearance of your book—intelligent design that matches content to form, quality paper and printing, and binding for longevity—I suggest that you'll want your book produced by a university press. A browse in a bookstore to compare university press and trade books as aesthetic and physical objects will prove my point.

Promoting and Marketing

A university press hopes at best to break even; a trade publisher is in the business to make money. In an eagerness to capitalize on the market for popular subjects—black studies, ecology, the women's movement—commercial publishers actively seek "trendy" manuscripts. The most important and ground-breaking work in these new areas of inquiry comes from scholars. Thus a trade publisher will reason that if a scholarly book is sufficiently readable, it just might appeal to the nonspecialist, that hard-to-define "general reader," and it just might sell enough copies to realize a profit. It is not uncommon, however, for trade publishers to overestimate this illusive general readership, to overprint books, and to "remainder" the leftovers after a year or two. Although they often lose money on these borderline scholarly-general books, trade publishers justify such works as prestige items that will establish their interest in the subject area and attract other, more popular, better-selling books to their lists.

Still, you might ask, isn't a trade publisher likely to spend more money on promotion and sell more copies of a book than a university press could? Yes and no. Trade publishers concentrate their promotional budgets on only a few books each season—those they hope will be big sellers and those with the greatest subsidiary-rights potential—in an effort to produce the income that will offset the losses they expect from the prestige items on their list. They probably will do more general space advertising of your book than a university press will. If university presses do not advertise lavishly in major media, it is because they have learned that these expensive ads do not sell books. Instead university presses make extensive use of constantly updated, specialized mailing lists to promote books to the most likely individual purchasers and to libraries. Trade publishers concentrate not on identifying and reaching the particular groups of interested readers but on advertising to general readers, few of whom buy scholarly books, even readable ones. Of course, like trade publishers, university presses also sell books to bookstores through sales representatives and to libraries through wholesalers. They advertise in scholarly journals and exhibit books at professional meetings. They send out innumerable review copies of new hardbacks and examination copies of paperbacks. While the trade publisher may sell more copies of your book to peripheral general readers than a university press will, a university press will know better who the primary readers and reviewers of your book will be, where they are, and how to reach them. And, unlike a trade publisher, a university press will keep your book in print for years and years.

Have I overstated my case for the university publisher? Possibly, since I am one. Yet over the years I've spoken to authors who have had their first books published by university presses and who have "gone trade," only to be disappointed in the editing, production, and marketing of their second books. It pays, I think, to be realistic about the nature of one's book. A scholarly book is a scholarly book, despite its popular trappings, and a scholarly book deserves the expert treatment of the people who are in business to publish scholarly books, university presses.

The Condition of Feminist Scholarship:
One Publisher's View

Tennessee has published more books by female authors in recent years than ever before; why have we not published more feminist scholarship? What has been wrong with the manuscripts of feminist scholars we have turned down? If I may generalize—and the space limitations of this article restrict me to generalizations—the most frequent complaints leveled against feminist scholarship have to do with balance, perspective, and tone. In a "Guest Word" article in the *New York Times Book Review* (8 Feb. 1976) Lionel Tiger, the Rutgers anthropologist, touched on these complaints when he objected to the trend of assigning books by and about women to female book reviewers. He warned of the danger of feminist scholarship's becoming a ghetto. And he hinted that male critics, when they do review books by women, seem reluctant to criticize the quality of the writing and research for fear of being accused of antifeminism. He went on to say, "In any social movement a shift must be made away from the unambiguous first flush of moral assertion to dispassionate analysis."

Although much of what Tiger was saying smacks of sour grapes, his call for a shift from moral assertion to dispassionate analysis points up what I have objected to in some feminist scholarship. Although passion and polemics have a place in social and political movements and in popular and journalistic writing supporting such movements, feminist scholarship *is* scholarship, and scholarship by definition is dispassionate analysis. It is not polemical. It does not begin with a thesis and choose or manipulate the evidence to fit the thesis. It assembles all the evidence and sifts it to find the thesis.

And scholarship is also good writing. Feminist critic Ann Douglas once commented:

> The feminist tone can be deluded, offensive. A number of intelligent women . . . seem to believe that, as women writing about women, they have accomplished something. Bad writing on slight subjects is of course endemic to the academic profession. This feminist self-inflation, however, is a different matter: it is the trust that, simply because one is in a new place, any step taken constitutes progress.

I believe in the validity of feminist scholarship both as a corrective to the biases of masculinist scholarship and as a cogent approach in its own right. I hope it will lead to a balanced scholarship, neither masculinist nor feminist, both male and female; in short, to fully humanistic scholarship. I am all the more disappointed, then, when feminist scholarship is less than excellent. But many of the feminist scholars I read are passionate, not dispassionate analysts. In their attempt to right wrongs, their ideology limits their perspectives, and they are sometimes as lopsided as the masculinist scholars they are trying to correct. For example, does it make sense for a feminist critic to compare male and female writers from the point of view of sexual socialization without discussing geographic, economic, historic, and other differences between them? The most prevalent criticism in readers' reports on manuscripts in feminist literary criticism can be summed up by this phrase from one report: "Ignores the socio-economic evidence her subject demands." The next most prevalent criticism has to do with tone—a tendency of some feminist scholars to campaign and moralize rather than to evidence, analyze, and convince.

Am I being too hard on feminist scholarship? Am I expecting an excellence in feminist scholars that I do not look for in traditional scholars? Because I am a woman, perhaps so. I am not saying that feminist scholarship has more or fewer faults than any other school of scholarship, but because of its newness it is controversial and it is more vulnerable to criticism than traditional kinds of scholarship are. To my mind, therefore, it has an obligation to prove itself. And it cannot prove itself unless it fulfills the established—yes, the established—criteria for excellence in scholarship. I think it is beginning to do so. Recent reviews indicate that feminist scholarship is coming of age. In readers' reports I see more statements like this one: "She possesses the rare ability to deal with and solve controversial problems without adopting a polemical tone." It offends me that this ability should be considered rare in feminist scholars, just as it incenses me that some publishers, in their eagerness to jump on the bandwagon and to capitalize on the faddish aspects of feminism, have published some shoddy feminist scholarship. Feminist scholarship cannot afford to be shoddy. It deserves to be the best.

Notes

1. Although the guidelines suggested here apply specifically to works of scholarship—since these are the essence of a university press list—they may be adapted to proposals to prepare bibliographies and other reference tools, critical editions, symposia, and translations as well. Proposals for anthologies, readers, and textbooks should be sent to appropriate text and trade publishers.
2. A helpful guide to university presses, including their editorial interests, book series, and journals, is the *AAUP Directory,* available from the Association of American University Presses, 1 Park Ave., New York, NY 10016.
3. See, e.g., William B. Harvey, "The Publishing Contract," *Scholarly Publishing,* 8 (1977), 229–314.
4. Symposia present complex problems to both the volume editor and the publisher. For guidance, see Cyril E. Black and Carol Orr, "E Pluribus Unum: Symposia and Publishers," *Scholarly Publishing,* 5 (1974), 145–52.
5. For an illuminating discussion of the difference between a dissertation and a book manuscript and suggestions for rendering the first into the second, see Eleanor Harman and Ian Montages, eds., *The Thesis and the Book* (Toronto: Univ. of Toronto Press, 1976). For guides to preparing a manuscript for submission see *A Manual of Style,* 12th ed. (Chicago: Univ. of Chicago Press, 1969); *MLA Handbook* (New York: MLA, 1977).
6. Most university presses require at least two outside readings of a manuscript in which they are interested. The choice of appropriate readers is critical to a fair evaluation of a manuscript, and editors make every attempt to select readers who not only know the field of the manuscript but will evaluate the work objectively and offer reasonable and constructive suggestions for revision. Not being scholars, however, and dealing with manuscripts in a variety of disciplines, editors cannot be expected to know all the branches of learning, let alone the twigs on the branches. Therefore, editors will welcome information from the author about her field, about other scholars working in the same area, and about readers who might exhibit biases against the method or approach of the book.

Publishing Opportunities Abroad (Particularly in France)

Jean A. Perkins

American scholars working in the field of the modern languages have a fundamental choice to make that will, in large part, determine their publishing opportunities. If the scholar writes in English, there are few foreign publishing houses willing or able to consider the manuscript. If the scholar writes in a foreign language, few American university presses will consider the manuscript. In addition, the increasing reluctance of American presses to typeset anything at all in a foreign language means that quotations may have to be translated into English before the book can be published. This sharp dichotomy is not as noticeable in journals as it is in book publishing, since the more specialized journals accept manuscripts in whatever language seems appropriate to the subject. Therefore I will not attempt to delineate the possibilities of publishing articles abroad but will concentrate on books.

The reference section of any college or university library will supply the basic tools needed to understand the publishing situation in any foreign country. The three-volume *Book Trade of the World*, published jointly in Hamburg, London, and New York, gives a general overview of the state of publishing in each country. It covers such basic facts as the price structure, retail trade, reviewing practices, and prizes, but it is not too helpful to a scholar trying to find out specific information about individual publishing firms. The information in *Book Trade* does, however, give a sufficiently clear idea of the general state of publishing in any country to enable the scholar to decide whether it is worthwhile to go any further. For instance, the 1972 edition lists a total of 319 French publishers doing more than FF100,000 business a year, of which 15 firms carry more than 50% of the titles published in any given year. The total number of titles in that year, including first editions, theses, and so on, was about 23,000, of which almost 600 fell into the general category of history and literary criticism. In contrast, some 1,800 German publishers put out more than 30,000 titles a year, but more than 71% of the German titles were published by only 239 publishers, the remaining publishers being responsible for no more than 21 titles per year each. In Germany, linguistics and literary history account for approximately 5% of the total number of titles per year.

Two other sources of information should be consulted before going to an individual book publisher's catalog to determine which publishing house is most likely to look with favor on a manuscript submitted from abroad. *Publishers' World* runs articles on publishing and quite frequently supplies recent information about changing policies of various publishing houses. And finally there is *Publishers' International Directory*, updated every two years, and a mainstay in the order department of any library. The first part of this directory has approximately thirty-thousand entries of publishing houses, listed by country and area of publishing interest:

DROZ S.A. Libraire Genève
Fict, Lit, Law, Ling, Econ.

"Lit" is the significant subject heading for our field and a convenient second section has a subject index listing names of publishers by country in a particular field.

Having extracted from these sources a list of publishing houses that might be interested in reviewing the manuscript, an author should then go directly to the catalogs that list the most recent titles and that usually indicate what has been and will be published. Sometimes a statement about editing policy is included. For example, some houses limit their titles to new editions of classic texts; some, to poetry. Each catalog gives a fairly clear idea of the various "Collections" that constitute the most likely publishing source for a specific title in that category. For instance, Minuit lists the following "Collections": Littérature, Arguments (reissues of important critical works), Critique, Le Sens Commun (in which we find Cassirer, *Substance and Fiction,* and Furet, *Lire et écrire*), Grands Documents (usually archival materials and critical editions), Revues and Autrement Dites (which publishes feminist materials). Collections that respond to the interest in women's studies are published by Table Ronde (Féminine), Gonthier (Femme),

Centurion (Femmes Actives), Cercle Bibliographique (Femmes Célèbres), Mondiales-Del Luca (Femmes Célèbres de l'Histoire) and
Grasset (Femmes dans la Vie). Editors of these series are usually
named, and the value of addressing a manuscript to a particular person
cannot be overestimated.

Obviously these steps must be informed by some knowledge not
only of the language but also of the field into which the manuscript
falls. Our individual knowledge about what has been published by
whom in the last few years may well be the best possible source of information. Since my own field is French literature and history of ideas
in the eighteenth century, I know that there are only a few publishing
houses in France that have brought out interesting works recently:
Belles-Lettres, Bordas, CDU-SEDES (Centre de Documentation Uni-
versitaire et Société d'Edition d'Enseignement Supérieur), Colin, Di-
dier, Droz, Editions Sociales, Firmin-Didot, Gallimard, Grasset,
Hachette, Hatier, Klincksieck, Lettres Modernes, Minuit, Mouton, Ni-
zet, Pauvert, Plon, PUF (Presses Universitaires de France), and Seuil.
Of these Gallimard and Hachette are large commercial firms that are
unlikely to be interested in a scholarly treatise, and, to my recollection,
only Droz and Klincksieck have published anything in English. So the
list narrows itself, as the French would say.

The PUF sometimes collaborates with American university presses
to publish scholarly works, but this pattern has by no means become
standard and thus two separate editorial boards must judge a manuscript. The PUF's editorial policy is stated as follows:

The PUF puts its major effort into publishing treatises, manuals,
theses, important works in which higher education and university
research are durably encased.

Few of the individual university presses in France, such as Grenoble,
Lille 3, and Provence, have published books in French by scholars who
are not members of the faculty of those universities. When they do, my
hunch is that the author is known to the members of the group of university faculty working on a particular problem at that university.
French research, even in a field such as literature, tends to be done by
teams, *équipes de chercheurs,* who collaborate in many ways, organizing conferences and congresses, publishing joint research efforts, and
supporting one another's research in informal ways. If one becomes
part of such a group, the opportunities for publishing abroad widen.
Otherwise it is rather a chancy affair, especially for a newcomer to the
field.

The French reliance on "Collections" puts a great deal of discre-
tionary power in the hands of a particular editor. Often there is no
editorial board, no anonymous submission to review, no general discus-

sion of whether the work would make a real contribution to the field, only a reading by a single editor who decides whether or not the work would fit into his or her particular collection, enhance its status, round out its coverage, and of course sell. The question of sales has always been of prime importance in French publishing, since there is nothing that corresponds to the type of subsidy that American university presses have enjoyed over the years. This element of sales is now becoming more important in the United States as well, since universities can no longer afford to subsidize their presses as heavily as they did during the "affluent sixties." But old habits die hard, and the mechanisms used to review manuscripts by American presses do give a newcomer a fairer chance at publication, although the more haphazard European system sometimes works better for certain types of scholarly works, especially those involving a new approach.

In December 1977 a new periodical entitled *A Paraître* published its first number with a special section entitled "Vie et Mort des Sciences Humaines" ("Life and Death of the Humanistic Sciences") (pp. 29–41). The journalist Barthélémy interviewed ten editors (9 men and 1 woman) representing Aubier-Montaigne, Bordas, Colin, Dunod, Gallimard, Gauthier-Villars, Klincksieck, Payot, PUF, Seuil. They paint a gloomy picture of the economic status of French publishing, commenting in particular on the absence of a proper method of subsidizing scholarly publication in France. For instance, they receive FF10,000 for each thesis published but estimate that each one costs at least FF50,000 to produce. The only sources of subsidy for scholarly works other than theses are the Centre National de Recherche Scientifique, which can subsidize only works of French origin, and the Centre National des Lettres, which only makes loans, to be paid back out of sales. Patrice Laurent, representing Klincksieck, noted that without these subsidies very little of a serious nature could be published in France; 10% of their books receive such a subsidy. François Wahl, of the Editions de Seuil, remarks that the public in France for such works is very small indeed; in Great Britain or the United States press runs of 5,000 to 8,000 can still be profitable; not in France. Jean-Max Leclerc of Editions Armand Colin clearly delineates the reliance a publishing house such as theirs has on the world of the university, which in the field of "Lettres et Sciences Humaines" has been steadily losing financial ground to both "Sciences Sociales" and "Sciences Naturelles." Only the PUF has the resources to do press runs of as few as 3,000 to 5,000 copies, and they publish about 400 titles a year, mostly in a series of 60 collections, including the well-known "Que sais-je?"

The differing habits of these various press editors lie buried in their answers to a series of set questions. The representative of Seuil states categorically that all their publication is now done through "Collections," which are entrusted to a single editor, and notes that they have a tendency to cultivate authors who are under contract with Seuil. Each of their collections publishes about thirty titles a year. Colin solicits manuscripts from authors publishing in the areas they are particularly interested in: philosophy, psychology, sociology, history, and geography. If manuscripts arrive unsolicited, they consult well-known authorities in the field (presumably university professors). More information about Klincksieck is available than about any of the other publishing houses. Patrice Laurent acknowledges that their major field of inquiry is linguistics, more particularly aesthetics, semiotics, and narratology. They have almost 60 different collections and find that 20% of their titles carry the financial load for the other 80%. Their editorial habits are clearly described: Klincksieck receives approximately one manuscript a day; 20% of the submissions are immediately rejected as not fitting into Klincksieck's sphere of interest; the others are "examined and read," and the final result is the publication of approximately 80 titles a year, that is, about 1 in 3. He notes that for editors of literary titles the ratio is about 1 in 10.

What stands out most clearly in this series of interviews is that literary criticism per se is not much in demand by French publishers. A few years ago linguistics was most in demand, and new collections still seem to be created in response to this phase. Pierre Nora of Gallimard points out that attaching oneself to such phases is fraught with peril:

I would venture to believe that there will be a tremendous proliferation in what are called the human sciences and that a large part of them will fall back into the classically typical university ghetto. Ten years ago there was a great rush to Linguistics that has already fallen off. Psychoanalysis and History are now on the crest of the wave and they'll also die down. (p. 38)

The names of authors most frequently mentioned by this group of editors are Barthes, Foucault, Genette, Lacan, Ladurie, and Sollers. If you subscribe to the school of one of these authors, your chances of being published in France are probably fairly good right now. If not, the American university presses remain a better choice, especially if you happen to fall into the hands of a good editor who will supply you with thoughtful critical evaluations of your work, either from himself or herself or from the group of specialist readers to which all manuscripts are submitted.

Scholarly Reprint Publishing*

Ralph Carlson

The Feminist Controversy in England, 1788–1810 is a hardback reprint series consisting of forty-four titles in eighty-nine volumes. Reproduced in photographic facsimile, the books are printed on acid-free, 250-year-life paper and bound with quality library bindings. From the end of the eighteenth century through the beginning of the nineteenth a great debate took place over the position women should occupy in society. The series editor, Gina Luria, has included the most important statements on both sides of the controversy and has contributed an introduction to each title, containing a biographical sketch of its author and a brief summary of the sociohistorical context in which the book was written. This series aims to provide anyone studying the history of the "woman question" with the major documents published during the period. The books sell for $50 per volume.

I work as an acquisitions editor for Garland Publishing and this is one of almost one hundred such series we have published to date, totaling over four thousand volumes. Does my description sound like a publisher's advertisement? Well, of course, it is. But it also demonstrates just what scholarly reprinting is all about. It describes the market, the format, the economics, the promotion, and the editing of such a series. Let's take each aspect in turn.

The market for the books reprinted by Garland and other scholarly reprinters is almost exclusively academic libraries. These reprints are

29

intended for primary research. They are not books that every scholar in the field would need in his or her personal library or that undergraduate courses would include on an assigned reading list. Thus they are published in the format most appropriate for libraries: quality hardback bindings and acid-free paper, with a life of 250 years. They are reprints of books that most libraries do not own. The originals of many reprints are, in fact, very rare. Garland once published a reprint for which there was no known complete original; we had to make up a complete copy from the copies held in three different libraries, each of which was missing pages.

Although there are some 1,700 academic libraries in the United States (not to mention the thousands of other academic libraries throughout the world), only a small percentage of these libraries purchase the average reprint series. Some libraries have tight budgets that must be spent only on new books and periodicals, others are primarily undergraduate libraries. Garland's first print runs on most series range from 150 to 250 copies. The lower limit is the point below which the manufacturing cost per copy becomes so great that the retail price would, we feel, be prohibitively high.

We hope to sell our first printing over a period of five to eight years. The Feminist Controversy series was announced in 1973, when we printed 150 copies of each title. At the end of 1981 we had sold an average of 126 copies of each title. If there is a greater demand for an individual title, more copies are printed. *Mary, a Fiction,* by Mary Wollstonecraft, one of the books in this series, has sold a total of 220 copies so far. Our best-selling series, a collection of contemporary reviews of British Romantic writers edited by Donald H. Reiman of the Pforzheimer Library, has sold over 700 copies to date. We have found that though libraries purchase most of our books, faculty members make most purchasing decisions. We therefore try to organize each series around a topic focused enough so that all the books will interest a scholar specializing in the area.

Reprints are sold primarily through catalogs mailed to faculty members and librarians. In most disciplines we must mail at least ten thousand catalogs to reach the potential market. Since the market for any single title is small and mailing costs are high, we publish reprints as a series of thematically related books rather than as single titles. If we had done a flier describing a single title in the Feminist Controversy series, it would have cost a minimum of $2,500 (10.9¢ each to mail, plus handling, printing, typesetting, and overhead costs) and the total sale (assuming we sold 150 copies at $50 each) would have been $7,500. Marketing expenses on a series of books are usually no more than 10% of sales, as opposed to over 30% in this example.

At Garland we prefer to have a minimum of fifteen to twenty books in a series, although a series with greater sales potential can certainly be smaller (the Reiman series has 10 volumes and was well worth doing). The upper limit on the size of a series is determined by how many titles merit reprinting. We have reprinted, for example, three related series of eighteenth-century novels, totaling 236 volumes, and they have sold quite well.

We believe that it is essential to have an academic editor for each series. A specialist can tell us, first of all, whether a reprint series should be done at all. It could be that the most important books on a topic remain in print, have been reprinted by another firm, or are already held by the libraries that would be the most likely customers. An ideal series editor will be thoroughly familiar with all the books that could be included in a series, will know their relationship to one another and to subsequent books, and will be able to choose those titles that are central to the topic. The editor will also know which edition of a given book is the best or most useful, or whether more than one edition should be included in the series. We pay our academic editors a royalty of five percent of the sales of books in their series and feel that their expertise is well worth this expense. (Editors are expected to pay research expenses, if any, themselves.) Of course, any two experts will disagree as to exactly what should be reprinted and, for each of our catalogs, we ask the series editor to spell out exactly why she or he has chosen a specific title and why it should be in a permanent library collection.

An important decision a reprint publisher faces with a new series is whether the books should have new introductions. It may be that a book or an author is so unknown that even other scholars in the field need an explanation of why this work was chosen for reprinting. Our rule of thumb at Garland is that, if introductions are appropriate, they should be relatively brief (1,000 to 2,000 words) and primarily biographical and bibliographical. They should tell what is known about the life of the author (if this information is relevant), how this title relates to the other titles in the series, and why this edition was chosen. The introduction should also give references to other materials that will clarify the importance of the work. We discourage extensive critical introductions in reprints. By the time a scholar has written several such essays, he or she has the groundwork for a critical work on the topic, much more appropriately published, we believe, as a book or an article.

I have discussed hardback reprinting because this is the format I know best (it is the only format published by Garland), but there are two other formats that are important to mention—paperback and microform. Paperback reprints are almost never purchased by libraries. They are published in the hope that they will be assigned classroom reading and, in addition, be sold through bookstores. They are usually published by paperback firms whose primary list consists of titles sold to the same market. Microform publication is usually reserved for large documentary collections, though more and more microform firms are publishing the type of material once published almost exclusively by hardback reprinters. There is no real reason why most if not all of the books that are now sold as hardback reprints couldn't be sold (and sold less expensively) in microform, except that most scholars and libraries still seem to prefer the more traditional book format. To scholars who have used books for their entire careers, film of any kind seems foreign—to be used only if absolutely necessary. And books are certainly portable in a way that the equipment needed for viewing microforms is not. I do think we will see more and more use of microform, but I also think the transition will be slow.

Let me close with a brief discussion of the two questions I am most frequently asked about reprint publishing—how do you choose the books you reprint, and why do you announce books before they are published?

Deciding what to reprint often comes down to choosing series editors. We concentrate on general fields that we believe will sell better than others will. Often we approach a potential editor and ask her or him to suggest a series to us. Or we decide that we want to do a series on a topic and set out to find the most appropriate editor. And we are always eager for unsolicited suggestions for series and for scholars to serve as series editors. Some of our best series have originated in this manner. Once we have chosen a series and an editor, we ask the editor to provide us with a list of titles. If we have any questions about the list or if the editor prefers to have the list reviewed (as often happens), we send it to scholars we all agree on. Sometimes the editor we have chosen is the foremost scholar in the field and there is no reason to have the list reviewed.

Every reprinter I know announces books before they are published. All publishers share one reason for following this practice: to generate interest in, and orders for, books before publication. But the special nature of reprinting also makes it virtually impossible to publish all the books in any given series before that series is announced. Let's take the Feminist Controversy as an example. Before the books could be sent to the printer, all eighty-nine volumes had to be ordered in microfilm (since no library would let us unbind the books to send to our printer) from a number of different libraries; the microfilm had to be printed up; introductions had to be written; missing and defective pages had to be replaced; front matter, including the introductions, had to be set in type. This process took well over a year and a great expenditure of staff time and money. This expenditure would simply have been too great to bear if we could not have published some of the books and started getting some return on them before the last book was ready. If we had published each book as it was ready to be sent to the printer and waited to announce the series until all the books were available, we would have had an enormous amount of money tied up in inventory—a financially untenable situation. So we announced the series when we were about to publish the first books and published the remainder of the volumes over the next year. Although this method of publication may cause problems for libraries, I don't see reprinters changing their operations. If you (or your library) need to know specifically when a book will be available, call the customer service department of the publisher collect. The publisher's representative can tell you if the book is published and, if it is not, whether it will be available within the next four to six months.

The long-range future of hardback scholarly reprint publishing is, to say the least, uncertain. As I indicated, more and more books will certainly be done in microform. Library acquisition budgets are being cut, and their purchasing power is dwindling with inflation. We at Garland believe, however, that there will continue to be a market for carefully chosen hardback reprints. We hope you agree.

Notes

*For a history of scholarly reprint publishing in the United States, as well as by far the best overview of the industry, see Carol A. Nemeyer's *Scholarly Reprint Publishing in the United States* (New York: Bowker, 1972).

Textbook Publishing
Some Notes on Responsibility

Ronald Mallis

Whatever our connection to education—instructor, author, student, publisher, administrator, or bewildered onlooker—we are caught in a cross fire generated by our colleagues, our professional obligations (sometimes ill-defined), our values (also vague), the media, the zeitgeist. In the face of this onslaught of the ephemeral and (perhaps worse) the trivial, we try to retain something of our sanity and some notion of what is or could be important.

For this reason and any number of other reasons, a writer writing about, for example, publishing and introductory English texts has to be cautious; even more important, his or her audience has to be skeptical. The subject almost invariably tends to freeze-dry the brain as the usual bromides are trotted out. In fact we many times seem to feel that we owe it to ourselves to have said it all before or to have heard it all before: worldliness as measured by the number of times we can shrug.

And yet . . .

Somewhere in the midst of this jungle of noise can be found the coherent signs of a few trails that require some further mapping—that demand more than a polite shrug. Specifically, we need to talk about a subject—the women's movement—that has managed so far—though not without struggle—to withstand its transformation into a forty-five-second spot on the evening news. We owe it to ourselves to investigate

35

where our responsibilities lie if we are to protect this phenomenon from the verbal detritus that constantly threatens to bury it.

I once offered an English instructor the opinion that the women's movement, carried to its logical conclusion, is potentially as revolutionary as anything uncovered by Darwin or Marx. There are, needless to say, many miles to go before the revolution. Until then, what do we do? What possible bearing can the movement have on the way we function professionally, whether as editors, writers, teachers, or students?

To attempt an answer requires some understanding of the context. As an English editor I served in a professional environment that is— and must be—marked by a constant tension between the imperatives of a profit-making, quality publisher and those of an educational system or series of subsystems. This relation—or ecology, more likely—is perhaps unique in the business world and certainly exhilarating. And, as with any such elegant and complex system, the needs and workings of one part invariably impinge on, and are in turn affected by, the needs and workings of other parts.

Even within so interlinked a system, however, each component has its own point of view. At their most rhapsodic, publishers feel themselves privileged to be able to make humankind's achievements generally available, to serve as a gazetteer to the world, informing it of what it has been doing. But these publishers do not function unilaterally—in fact cannot function unilaterally, else they would remain in business for about as long as it once would have taken me to clean out my desk. They must act in closest consort with their audience and simultaneously with those who provide the content of their business—with, in short, the market.

Publishers at times talk about "the market" as if it were a coherent entity, a single object whose transformations are predictable in their unpredictability. In point of fact, because publishers work with the educational process and because process by definition involves both known and unknown variables, many of the publishers' conclusions may be annoyingly tentative. Using whatever intelligence and sensitivity and bravery they can muster, however, they try to perceive the dim outlines of a trend, they try to generalize from the mote of the particular, they try to use the plural as often as possible, hoping the singular won't notice. And they try to draw some reasonable conclusions.

These conclusions—drawn from a reading of the market—provide publishers with certain guidelines that, though somewhat elastic, are relatively tight and clearly demarcated. These guidelines in turn are formed at least in part by the actions of those who teach and those who are being taught. To one degree or another, each knows what is possible and what is necessary. A publisher's major responsibility, then, is to help others realize those possibilities and to make available the fulfillment of those necessities.

In one of my earlier incarnations, I attended, as geography editor, an evening session of a national convention. I heard publishers berated for what were perceived to be racist textbooks (not sexist, mind you; this, after all, was the late sixties). A motion was made to boycott all books by publishers so accused. Not wishing to excuse any form, however slight, of racial prejudice and acknowledging that virtue was as rare a commodity within a publishing house as anywhere else, I still had to point out that these same texts were, many of them, written by people attending the convention and used in startling numbers by a rather large percentage of their colleagues. It was probably at this time that I became aware of the ecology that defined our professional lives—positively for most, negatively for some. And it began to occur to me that publishers cannot operate in a vacuum and then be blamed because the vacuum exists.

To move a bit closer to home, how many instructors now teaching literature refuse to admit to the existence, to paraphrase Woolf, of Shakespeare's sister? At what point will "women's lit" and "minority lit" disappear from the curriculum and reappear as part of a more general investigation of humankind's intellectual achievement? On whose instructions were the "standard" nineteenth-century American authors made standard? At what point will copy editors be able to stop counting the number of masculine versus feminine pronouns and simply assume an author is being realistic in the true sense of the word? At what point will freshman writing texts be void of examples that portray "girls" as little angora-sweatered pincushions and "boys" as minimachos?

Admittedly these are rhetorical conceits—not really questions as much as muffled calls for action. Other, more fundamental questions quickly move them off center stage: To what extent will the renewed interest in literature by women influence the way in which drama, for example, is presented to an introductory class? Can we use the standards derived from Western literary criticism to judge the literature that criticism has so conscientiously excluded from its considerations? Are we merely (sic!) adding more writers to the certified roster, or are we suggesting a more general reevaluation of genres? Do we now begin to pay more attention to mythic and sexual archetypes? If any of these are valid questions, at what point do the answers become part of the educational mainstream? Or, put another way, when and how will the market shift? Who is to provide the answers and how are they to be provided? I'm not about to prejudge the answer to the first part of the last question; this is, after all, a democracy. As to the last part, I can perhaps suggest a few avenues.

A commercial publisher receives each day a sobering number of manuscripts, partial manuscripts, proposals, queries, ideas sketched on clouds—some sign that someone somewhere wants to publish a book. Almost automatically, an editor performs a kind of triage on these submissions: the disorganized, the poorly conceived, the monographs, the bizarre expressions of a most peculiar approach to a particular course are immediately rejected. Those that appear as though they might have something to say (and what they say usually turns out to be a not-so-faint echo of dozens of their predecessors) are put aside for the time being. And those that, for one reason or another, resonate in some way are acted on immediately.

How, of course, does a proposal "resonate"? How does an editor, after having talked with perhaps a dozen or more people on any particular day on any particular campus, recognize, amidst the verbiage, something of value? Well, for one thing, the potential writer manages to articulate certain educational goals beyond his or her own self-improvement. This writer seems as well to have some understanding of the broader educational market that again goes beyond his or her own classes and those of his or her own three best friends. This writer wants to talk about why his or her own book will be attractive to a representative instructor and a representative student at a representative campus. In short, the proposed book has been designed to meet a need that is definite and broad. As for those proposals put aside for a while, one looks at them and reads them and rereads them and gradually begins to wonder why the person bothered. There's nothing, after all, particularly wrong with any of them, but there's nothing particularly original about them either. I am not suggesting that a would-be writer engage in sudden shock tactics; I am suggesting that originality comes from an inherent integrity in the manuscript, from some specific sense of an author's commitment to his or her subject and to his or her audience, from some understanding of the larger educational environment.

Having assured myself that I had a proposal with at least the hint of quality about it, I would request a number of outside opinions from instructors who are teaching the course for which the book is designed. These reviewers were, presumably, people I knew (or had heard about) and trusted, people who represent a range of schools and who, depending on the specific proposal, are first-rate scholars and/or first-rate teachers. I would ask these reviewers to comment on a number of questions: Does the content of the proposed book seem to parallel the content of their courses? Are there any glaring omissions? Is the organization, at least based on the table of contents, balanced? How does the book relate to those already published for the same course? What are its major strengths? its weaknesses? Would these reviewers, finally, recommend such a book for adoption in their courses?

After securing a favorable response and ensuring that the economics of the project meet corporate requirements, an editor can presumably make a publishing offer. As an altogether important aside, I should add that before expressing interest, the editor will make certain that the proposed book is in an area for which he or she wishes to publish. Often, regardless of a book's seeming worth, an editor will know immediately that his or her list could not possibly sustain yet another introduction to literature. Thus from the author's point of view it becomes partially a question of being in the right place at the right time.

What I've described in admittedly coarse outline is a procedure no different for a freshman rhetoric text than it would be for a twentieth-century American literature anthology: quality is, after all, quality.

And, perhaps more to the point here, quantity is quantity. To reiterate what I've said earlier in a somewhat different way, a publisher cannot publish for a market that doesn't exist. Only rarely can a publisher create a market; more likely, a publisher can, at best, address creatively a market that is already there in some perceivable form. And if we add to this axiom the corollary that in order to remain even modestly profitable, a medium-sized publisher must in general realize nearly $100,000 in net income from the first-year sale of a new book, market size becomes even more of an issue.

Let's take this a step further, then, and say that market size—or market demand—is the final factor determining whether a book will be published. How is this demand created and made known to publishers? How can publishers be made to respond to social and intellectual forces? We come, I think, back to our original notion of responsibility and to that finely tuned ecological system I talked about earlier.

Publishers and everyone else are now engaged in playing a kind of catch-up ball, with all the hysteria and anxiety that implies. A few Ms.'s. here, obeisance to Edith Wharton or Tillie Olsen or Ntozake Shange there, nothing too drastic, mind you, and we're all set. And so it will continue to be for the next several years.

I was fortunate, during my career as English editor, in having been able to put under contract a number of anthologies dealing specifically with women and minority writers. I don't, however, feel particularly self-righteous. I insist that further, and perhaps more important, changes must come from those who are teaching—not necessarily at the preeminent schools and not necessarily among a relatively small coterie whose views I am probably not challenging. Were I still an editor I would want demands made on me and I would want to be able to respond to those demands in a way that did honor to all that has been achieved. I would want to be able to say with confidence that our putative market will not be dismayed by the sight of a few playwrights who have not been included in every other anthology. Unfortunately, today the dismay is real; to stay in business a publisher must acknowledge it.

As I've said, none of us has any reason to feel self-righteous or self-satisfied. We must recognize our individual responsibilities; we must recognize the limits, real or not, of our respective professions; we must do more than talk to ourselves. Otherwise we will remain stymied, nothing will change, the same tired old territory will engender even more fatigue and even more cynicism, and the new sounds we now hear will simply fade into the cacophony of the cross fire.

Boards and Paper
Feminist Writing and
Trade Publishing

Martha M. Kinney

Time was when a book, to be a book, had to be bound in hard bindings of cloth over boards with Smyth-sewn signatures of rag paper over which, if you ran your finger, you would detect the impression of the foundry type that had printed the words on the page. Likely as not the book had been set in type and proofread by someone who could both read and spell. Time was when a cup of coffee cost a nickel, a gallon of gas could be had for four bits, and no one had ever heard of Rosemary Rogers' *Sweet Savage Love.* But times do change, in book publishing no less than in other aspects of American life.

Within the last ten years changes that began to affect the book business after World War II have accelerated to create an industry that only faintly resembles its former self.[1] The emergence of the paperback as a widely accepted book format, the waning popularity and affordability of the hardcover book in the trade market, the trend toward merging smaller publishers into media conglomerates, and the increasingly treacherous economics of publishing in times of double-digit inflation all have seriously threatened to alter the nature of what gets published and what the public reads. Because book publishing is a low-profile industry, few people outside understand the implications of these changes. Some would argue, and I include myself among them, that these changes have created an environment hostile to the best interests of writers and readers. As E. L. Doctorow noted in a *New York*

Times Op-ed page editorial, "The structure of book publishing has changed. . . . The concentration into fewer and fewer hands of the production and distribution of literary work is *by its nature* constricting to free speech and the effective exchange of ideas and the diversity of opinion."[2] This change poses a particular challenge to scholars, teachers, and students, who are among the first to be affected by a publishing industry less willing and able to respond to their needs. If teachers and scholars of women's studies clearly understand the nature of these developments in book publishing, they will be better equipped to influence publishers to serve their needs.

Cheap paperback reprints of hardcover best-sellers have been around since the late 1930s, but the paperback book did not come into its own until after World War II. In the years following the war, a number of publishers began to rely on the magazine distribution network to sell paperbacks. The wholesale distributors placed cheap paperbacks on newstands and in corner drug, grocery, and variety stores across the country and soon could guarantee a national market for rack-sized paperbacks. Tens of thousands of readers came to rely on paperback books for information and entertainment. The big break for paperbacks, however, came in the late fifties, when less expensive paperback books began to displace more expensive hardcover textbooks in school and university classrooms. Publishing houses like New American Library produced lines of quality paperback books, such as Mentor Books and Signet Classics, that included both original and reprinted works of nonfiction and classic fiction that were appropriate for classroom adoption. Teachers who had resisted paperbacks as unfit for educational use discovered that they could assign up to ten paperbacks for the price of a single hardcover text. In addition, they could teach a range of points of view with more up-to-date material. Hosts of students grew up reading paperbacks in school and buying them to create affordable personal libraries. Future generations of paperback buyers were thus ensured.

During the early sixties, hardcover trade publishers began to realize that paperbacks held great potential for expansion and profit as paperback sales eclipsed hardcover sales in terms of both dollars and units. In the boom days of the sixties war economy, paperback sales, as well as hardcover sales to schools and libraries, were stimulated and supported by a liberal Democratic Congress and the federal funds it earmarked specially for the purchase of instructional and reading material—chiefly books. Librarians and teachers learned then that the purchase of paperback books could stretch those government dollars. Also, the social unrest and political protest movements of the sixties produced any number of documents, manifestos, and artifacts of counterculture that found a completely compatible medium in the paperback book. As *The Whole Earth Catalogue* took shape in an oversized paperback format, with what now seems a ridiculously low price of $4.95, so much information was crammed into four-hundred odd pages of newsprint that it truly was a revolutionary book and created a new degree of acceptance for the large format paperback.

Paperbacks have succeeded over the last thirty years because they have enormous appeal. They are more widely available, portable, disposable, and, most important, affordable. In the fifties, quality paperback editions of all of George Eliot's works were available from Pocket Books for prices between 35¢ and 50¢ and hardcover trade books were selling at cover prices of between $3.95 and $5.95. With the price of a paperback book less than ten percent of the price of a hardcover, it's easy to understand why paperbacks were so successful in capturing a large market. During the late sixties and early seventies, the price difference between hardcover and paperback grew larger as hardcover prices moved upward at a faster pace than paperback prices. Inflated production costs, particularly in the price of paper and labor, coupled with smaller print runs over which these costs could be distributed, forced hardcover publishers to increase prices, making their books less attractive to book buyers and uncompetitive with cheaper paperbacks. By the late seventies the economics of hardcover publishing had become terribly difficult as the costs of production continued to climb steadily and threatened to make hardcover books luxuries for all but the very devoted or the very rich. As Victor Tempkin, a seasoned publishing executive long associated with Bantam Books and now president of Berkley/Jove, remarked in an article in the *New York Times Book Review*:

> The whole industry has changed. Fifteen years ago it was very hard to lose money on a book. Then it got to the point where seven out of 10 books were mistakes. But that was all right. The three winners would make up for the seven losers. That won't work anymore. The margins are worse, the competition is tougher. You have to make less mistakes. This business has gotten to be like Hollywood, with the glamour of Hollywood and the big money being paid like Hollywood. The trouble is, it's not a Hollywood type of business.[3]

Tempkin's comment specifically concerns mass-market publishing, but his observations apply equally to the entire industry. The situation he describes is complicated by the rather conservative pricing policies of publishers, who are by and large reluctant to raise the cover prices of books. Sometimes a publisher will underprice a book and take a loss on a first printing rather than price the book according to the prevailing profit-and-loss formula and risk pricing it out of the market. The publisher hopes to launch the book so well that it finds its readership at the lower price and, once it's established and selling, to raise its price to a more realistic and profitable level, making up the initial loss on subsequent printings.

The economics of book publishing are made more tortured by the antiquated custom of selling books on consignment. Publishers have long suffered from this policy of allowing booksellers to return unsold books for full credit—in some cases more than a year after publication. Hardcover books that are not sold from the shelves of bookstores within months may be packed up and returned to the publisher's warehouse for full credit. The same policy applies to paperbacks: if they fail to sell, sometimes within days, they may, according to their trim size, be either returned as full copies or stripped of their covers and shredded, with only the covers returned to the publisher, again for full credit. In hard times, when cash is scarce, booksellers find it tempting to pay their bills by returning slower-moving backstock titles, and hardcover returns have increased at an alarming rate.[4] There are moves afoot in the industry to end this expensive and wasteful policy and, instead, to sell books on a nonreturnable basis at higher discounts. David Godine has sold Nonpareil Books, his paperback line, on this basis quite successfully, and recently a major trade publisher, Harcourt Brace Jovanovich, Inc., attempted unsuccessfully to enforce a nonreturnable sales policy for their entire trade list.

Early in the history of paperback books, the larger hardcover publishers recognized the advantages of offering their authors the option of both hardcover and paperback editions. These publishers created new lines of paperback books, such as Doubleday's Anchor Books, Scribner's Library, and Random House's Vintage Books, which they sold to bookstores along with their hardcover lists.[5] The paperback lines made inroads into the traditionally exclusive hardcover market, but they did not become a force in the marketplace until the trade-paperback boom of the seventies, when a wide variety of hardcover and paperback publishers began to reckon with the demand for trade paperbacks. Hardcover publishers beefed up their dormant trade-paperback lines by acquiring more commercial books and spending handsome amounts of money to advertise and promote the books and the imprints to booksellers and book buyers. A larger share of the paperback market became so desirable and necessary to growth that some hardcover publishers, those large enough to afford it, acquired mass-market publishers available for takeover and staked a direct claim to the mass-paperback market. Across the industry almost every publisher who decided to acquire and publish a book found it necessary to consider the prospects for a paperback edition of the title. Hardcover editors were required to cast an eye much more frequently toward the paperback and especially the mass-paperback market, determined to publish books that stood a good chance of succeeding there. If the proposed book couldn't make it as a paperback, it might never find its way into print.

While trade publishers were paying closer attention to the paperback market, big business was growing more interested in publishing. Indeed, perhaps the most significant change in the publishing industry in recent years has been the growing trend toward conglomerates. Since the earliest days of book publishing the industry has thrived as a collection of small, independent enterprises. Often family-held companies, publishers were free to choose to publish a book strictly for its merit. Of course those houses who published only distinguished books had trouble keeping the lights on, but most houses banked on one or two strong-selling titles a season to pay the bills and underwrite less salable but significant books. Over the course of the last twenty years, these smaller, independent publishing houses have one by one been taken over by larger corporations capable of merchandising books worldwide and exploiting book properties simultaneously in several subsidiary markets: paperback, film and television, and foreign rights.

The high degree of concentration within book publishing becomes immediately evident when one considers that within the last twenty years twelve major media conglomerates have been created, until today there are few independent publishers of note, with the exception of Farrar, Straus & Giroux, Houghton Mifflin, and W.W. Norton. In 1979, the 13 largest publishing firms had total estimated sales of $3.72 billion (out of estimated industry-wide sales of $6.3 billion, or 59% of all book-publishing sales). In the same year, 8 publishing houses accounted for more than 50% of all "general interest" book sales. Of equal significance is that 89% of all mass-market paperbacks sold in the United States in 1979 were published by 11 companies,[6] and 10 of these 11 are subsidiaries of great American or international media conglomerates. (See Chart 1, in which the major conglomerates are listed in alphabetical order and the top ten mass-market publishers in bold face.)

Several of these conglomerates control companies that produce motion pictures, television programs, musical records, and tapes. Some of the larger and more diversified conglomerates own subsidiary companies that manufacture television sets, frozen dinners, carpets, or fine china. They are managed by business executives who produce and sell name brands in their manufacturing sectors and who bring expectations of efficiency and profit to book publishing. While these men and women have helped to improve business practices in a traditionally lax and inefficient industry, their business school mind-set tends to base publishing decisions largely on calculations of profitability and thus to have a damaging effect on the quality of books. Few editors or publish-

Chart 1
Major Media Conglomerates[7]

Bertelsmann
   Bantam Books. Recent joint venture with William Morrow (Perigord Press) to acquire titles for hardcover and mass market
   American Circle Book Club

CBS
   Fawcett
   Fawcett Marketing (national distributor of magazines and paperbacks)
   Holt, Rinehart & Winston
   CBS Network: television stations; magazines; video-discs

Doubleday
   Delacorte; Dial: **Dell Publishing;** Dell Distributing, Inc. (magazines and paperbacks); Literary Guild and other book clubs
   Motion pictures; printing and binding

Filmways
   Grosset & Dunlap; **Ace Books** (utilizes Publishers Distributing Corp. as national distributor)
   Magazines; motion pictures; television production

Gulf & Western
   Simon & Schuster; **Pocket Books**
   Pocket Books Distributing Corp. (national distributor of magazines and paperbacks)
   Paramount Pictures

Harper & Row
   Colophon Books, Perennial Library
   J.B. Lippincott & Co. (T.Y. Crowell and Lippincott trade titles now appear under the Harper & Row imprint); Basic Books; Ballinger Publishing Co.

Hearst Corp.
   Avon Books (utilizes International Circulation Distributors as national distributor); Arbor House Publishing Co., Inc.
   Newspapers

MCA
   G.P. Putnam; **Berkley/Jove Publishing Group** (utilizes International Circulation Distributors as national distributor); Coward, McCann & Geoghegan
   Universal Pictures; video-discs

Newhouse Publications
   Random House; Pantheon; Alfred A. Knopf; **Ballantine**, Fawcett
   Newspapers; major magazine publisher (Conde Nast); cable TV; pay TV

Time, Inc.
   Little, Brown; Book-of-the-Month Club; Quality Paperback Book Club
   Time and other magazines; Time-Life Books
   Motion pictures; *Washington Star;* cable TV (A.T.C.-2nd largest); H.B.O. (#1 in Pay TV-75 percent of the market)

Times-Mirror Corp.
  New American Library; Harry N. Abrams; New American Library Distributing (national distributors)
  Major magazine publisher; television broadcasting; cable TV; newspapers including *L.A. Times,* Long Island's *Newsday* and *Hartford Courant*

Warner Communications
  Warner Books; Warner Publisher Services (national distributor of paperbacks and magazines)
  Warner Brothers films; Warner-Annex cable TV; pay TV

ers would argue that a book should not pay for itself; however, the expectation that each and every title should not only pay for itself but also return a profit upwards of ten percent is a drastic change from the state of affairs ten to twenty years ago and poses a threat to future publication of works of invention and high quality.

The growth of the paperback industry, the concern with profitability, the influence of conglomerate-think, and the resulting effort to market and merchandise books like plastic razors or frozen dinners have altered the way books are sold to bookstores and the public. Because store buyers must see so many sales representatives in a single selling season and because publishers' representatives call on most accounts only two or three times a year, representatives have little time to present their long list of new titles and must make their sales pitch at a clip. Although this pattern occurs most frequently in the mass market, books are too often treated like packaged goods, promoted and sold by their "handles" to a mass audience, an audience persuaded by the image, a market of mediocrity. The "handle" or sales pitch a publisher's salesperson makes to the bookstore buyer reduces the content of a book to a sentence or two and answers the questions of why and for whom the book is being published. The "package" is the combined effect of the cover design, title, subtitle, and front and back cover copy. Ideally, the cover art and descriptive copy play off each other, creating a single strong impression intended to persuade the potential buyer to select a particular book from a field of titles. By slick packaging and pitching books are sold to distributors, bookstores, and ultimately to readers.

The danger in publishing, as in so many other areas of American life, is that profit will be allowed to take preeminence over other values. The bottom line of a profit-and-loss sheet based on estimated costs and anticipated sales can determine which author's work and what ideas get into print. When profit is the criterion, books with ideas or forms ahead of their time may be passed over for publication because only a few thousand people can be relied on to buy, read, and appreciate the work on its initial appearance. As we know from the publishing histories of some of our most splendid works of literature, initial reaction to a work has little to do with its long-term meaning, value, and ultimate success. But when publishers reject works of quality and complexity in favor of less worthy books, they impoverish us all and diminish our culture.

Against this background it is important to understand that the attitudes of publishers toward women's studies materials have been greatly influenced by their experience with the black studies market of the late sixties and early seventies. In the late sixties, educational and paperback publishers responded with enthusiastic support to the demand for black studies materials, in part because they were sympathetic to the aims of the civil rights movement. In larger part, however, they responded because they needed to identify and develop new educational markets at the college level, where market analysts were forecasting a drop in text sales as the young women and men of the postwar baby boom finally completed their education. The new curriculum for black studies created an instant need for new texts, a welcome development for publishers. But some of those who jumped on the bandwagon found that they had overreacted, commissioning series that duplicated other work and issuing texts for courses that would never be taught. By the late seventies the bubble had burst, not only in black studies but in many other areas of higher education. The civil rights movement had lost momentum, school and university enrollments were dropping, and federal funding was withdrawn from many programs. Black studies departments were merged with other disciplines and sometimes dissolved, courses were dropped from department listings, and instructors were terminated as their contracts expired. Many publishers found themselves with lists of undistinguished, unsalable titles and files of unfulfilled contracts for books scheduled for publication years too late. Because of this costly experience, publishers approached the women's studies market with greater caution. But unlike the black studies market, which proved to be almost entirely based on school and university adoptions with small support from bookstore sales, the women's studies market has been able to rely not only on academic adoptions but also on a large and stable audience of women readers. Women as a group buy and read more books than do blacks as a group. This is no biased observation; it is simply true that in terms of population statistics, women constitute 53% of the population while blacks constitute 10%. And as the Book Industry Study Group reported in 1979, most book readers and buyers are women and 25% of nonreaders are black.[8] The support of women readers, along with the influence of an ongoing feminist movement, created in the seventies an extraordinary decade of continuous and impressive publishing for and about women.

Since about 1968, when the feminist movement reemerged as a national issue, there has been an unprecedented flow of titles published exclusively for the women's market—that is, the feminist market, not the mainstream women's market of "sweet savage schlock" (once tame romances and Gothics, but in the seventies the domain of Rosemary Rogers and Kathleen Woodiweiss, whose formulas for success include an obligatory seduction every 2 to 4 pages). This truly rich period of feminist publishing was the result of hard work by dedicated women at all levels of publishing. Women writers found their voices and began producing manuscripts as never before on all aspects of women's experience. Women editors in publishing houses encouraged and supported women writers and argued with predominantly male sales managers and publishing boards for the right to publish feminist books. In their determination to enlarge the outlets for women's writing, women have also successfully established their own small presses and edited new journals. But perhaps the single most important reason for this splendid decade of women's books is that there is a readership that has bought and continues to buy the books, a strong and steady audience of women readers and university students, teachers and scholars.

The 1979–80 *Subject Guide to Books in Print* lists 22 pages of titles relating to women and women's experience, and of those approximately 3,300 titles more than 65% are available in inexpensive paperbound editions. Most of these books were first published in hardcover editions and later reprinted in either quality trade-paperback or mass-market paperback nine to twelve months after their initial publication. Some were issued simultaneously in hardcover and trade paperback, with the small quantity of hardcover books published essentially for reviewers and libraries and with the bulk of the print run going into the paperback edition. A smaller percentage were issued as original trade or mass-market paperbacks with no hardcover edition.

Every publisher in today's marketplace can publish in either hardcover or paperback. For instance, Nancy Friday's best-selling *My Mother, My Self* was first published in hardcover by Delacorte Press and a year later issued in a mass-market edition by Dell Books. Both Dell and Delacorte are owned by Doubleday. Another example is Dorothy Dinnerstein's *Mermaid and the Minotaur*, which Harper and Row published first in a hardcover edition and later, after trying to auction the book to paperback reprinters who found the book too challenging to risk a bid, decided to publish in their own trade-paperback line. *My Mother, My Self* was published in a mass-market format and distributed through wholesale as well as retail accounts because the hardcover was a best-seller and the market for a cheaper paperback edition was obviously quite large. Dinnerstein's book, a more specialized and serious work, sold modestly in hardcover; it was expected to appeal to a more limited audience in paperback; hence it was issued in a trade-paperback format and distributed through retail bookstores. In yet another example, Bantam Books, the long-time leader among paperback publishers, worked the equation the other way and issued its first hardcover book, Tom Robbins' *Still Life with Woodpecker,* simultaneously in both a trade and a mass-market edition. Because of Bantam's experience with Robbins' earlier novel, *Even Cowgirls Get the Blues,* which placed on both the mass-market and trade-paperback best-seller lists, Bantam was confident that Robbins' audience would support three simultaneous editions.

The differences between hardcover and paperback books are obvious in price, format, quality of binding and paper, and the size of the potential market. Hardcover and trade-paperback books share more characteristics than either does with mass-market paperbacks: they are both distributed primarily through retail bookstores in larger formats, at higher list prices, and in smaller quantities than mass-market paperbacks. There are few generic differences between hardcover and paperback books, although quality fiction, poetry, drama, critical works, and biography in addition to general nonfiction tend to be published in hardcover and trade paperback, while commercial fiction, genre novels, and popular nonfiction are published in mass-market paperback. Of course, there are exceptions, such as Avon's trade-paperback editions of the novel *Shanna* and the useful nonfiction guide *The People's Pharmacy.* Both of these books were distributed through the mass-market distribution system and could just as easily have been published in the smaller mass-market format; seeing their potential for profit, however, the publisher charged a considerably higher cover price for the book in a larger format.

It may be useful to scholars and writers who are shaping projects for publication to compare the physical, generic, and marketing distinctions among book formats. The chart that follows attempts to make clear at a glance the primary distinctions within trade-book publishing among hardcover, trade-paperback, and mass-market paperback books. It may also suggest possible paths to follow in proposing projects to publishers or in recommending out-of-print or public-domain titles for reprinting. At the least, it will demystify the formats and markets to help you better identify and reach your audience.

There are several points to keep in mind when proposing a project to a publishing house. Publishing is a paper-intensive industry, and most editors' desks are flooded with paper. It is an act of charity to query a publisher as to her or his interest in considering your project before you send a typescript or old edition or sample chapter. The best approach to an editor is through a one-page inquiry letter. Well conceived and well executed, a letter can be most effective in eliciting an invitation to submit sample material. Your letter should include a one-

Chart 2

Format (and examples)	Trim Size (in inches)	Cover Price (in dollars)	Print and Rerun Quantity	Genres	Means of Distribution	Outlets	Time in Print
Hardcover *The Women's Room; The Mermaid and the Minotaur; Women and Nature*	8¼ x 5½; 9⅝ x 6⅜	8.95–19.95	5,000–25,000 reruns: 3,000–10,000	all: fiction, poetry, drama, short story collections, criticism, biography, all nonfiction	publisher's salaried or commissioned representatives sell list regionally to bookstores	bookstores, department store book departments, libraries	through first printing: usually one to two years
Trade paperback *The Mermaid and the Minotaur; Our Bodies, Our Selves; Willa Cather*	8 x 5⅝	2.95–9.95 with illustrations: 9.95–14.95	7,500–75,000 reruns: 3,000–15,000	quality fiction; specialized nonfiction; poetry; drama; criticism; oversized titles	same as above	bookstores, chain stores (for selected titles), some libraries	through several printings: 3 to 5 years
Mass Market paperback *The Women's Room; My Mother, Myself; The Awakening*	4⅜ x 7	1.50–3.95	25,000–1 million reruns: 15,000–100,000	commercial fiction and nonfiction	regional wholesalers and jobbers, direct field force	bookstores, chain stores, wholesaler-served racks in newsstands, grocery stores, drug stores, variety stores, airports, terminals	most commercial fiction and nonfiction must sell 25,000 copies a year; educational books 2,500–5,000 copies a year to remain in print.

or two-paragraph description of the project, a statement of your ratio-
nale in proposing it, a description of your audience, a brief survey of
the competition, and an estimate of the size of the market. You should
also include an estimate of the length of the text in words or pages, the
length of time it will require to complete, and pertinent details about
yourself, such as whether and what you have published previously. For
instance, if you are proposing an anthology of readings for classroom
use, it will be important for you to identify the types of courses that
would likely adopt the text, to comment on competing books and spec-
ify how your proposed anthology is different and better, and to calcu-
late a possible annual sale based on the number of courses offered in a
year times the number of students who could be expected to enroll.

The potential backlist sale is an important consideration in the publisher's decision to take on a project. The collection of titles that continue to sell in quantity year after year really supports book publishing;
because inventory is expensive to warehouse, however, publishers do
demand a certain sales pace to keep a title in print. A book must pay
for its warehouse space and under the best conditions contribute to
the flow of income. Different publishers have different requirements
for keeping books in print, but in general hardcover books with annual
sales of between 800 and 1,000 copies will continue in print. Trade paperbacks are required to sell between 2,000 and 5,000 copies a year,
depending on the publisher, and mass-market titles must sell close to
20,000 copies a year to earn the right to a continued life in print. Of
course, publishers will always make exceptions for books, perhaps because of an ongoing relation with an author or the expectation of a re-
vived interest in a subject or writer.

I want to emphasize the importance of educating editors about the
size of the academic market. Editors work under intense pressure to
publish profitable books; most are desk-bound in New York and publish primarily for the retail bookstore market that they know best. In
general they know little about the market for women's studies and
need information about the potential long-term backlist sale for books
you propose in women's studies or in other growing disciplines.

Just as a book has a better chance for success when it can be target-
ed to a particular market, so will you have a better chance in placing
your project if you target a few publishers whose lists seem appropriate for the project you have in mind. If your book is aimed primarily at
an academic audience or is designed for classroom use, approach an
academic or textbook publisher. But if you are writing a more general
book for a larger lay readership, approach a trade publisher. Check
your bookshelves or, better yet, consult *The Literary Market Place,* a
key reference for the book industry (published by R. R. Bowker, available at the reference desk of your library) and make a list of publishers.

In *LMP* you will find both information about what each house publishes and the address of the publisher and the names of the senior editorial staff. You will increase your chances for a response if you address your inquiry letter to a particular editor. If the editor's catalog copy is written, the season's sales conference is past, and the next five-hundred-page manuscript isn't due for a couple of months, you can expect an answer to your query in two to three weeks. If a month passes and you have yet to receive a response, drop the editor a note with a copy of your earlier letter to jog her or his memory. If after a few more weeks you haven't had an answer, a phone call is in order. If the editor responds positively, she or he will ask you to submit an outline with two or more sample chapters. If you are invited to submit material to several publishers, be certain to inform each publisher that your work is being considered at the same time at another publishing house. This is a courtesy to an editor, who would be justifiably angry to discover after weeks of work shepherding a project through the house that an author had accepted an earlier offer from someone else. Depending on an editor's schedule it may be one to two months before you receive word of a decision. In that time the editor will have read your material and if she or he liked it, will have passed it along to colleagues with a request for their opinions. After two or three favorable readings, you may be asked to submit additional material for further consideration. If the publisher feels confident of your ability to deliver the book you propose, however, your project will be discussed at an editorial meeting and a decision made about whether to offer you a publishing contract. At this point marketing issues are raised and tentative formats, print orders, and prices are set, on which production estimates are based, and within a week or so a profit-and-loss sheet is prepared for the book to project the costs of various publishing options and indicate a dollar range for the advance against royalties that the publisher may offer. With a little luck, a book contract may be negotiated in three or four months; nine months to a year following acceptance of the delivered manuscript the project will finally have taken the shape of a finished book.

The agenda for the women's movement and for women's studies in the eighties must include a continued effort to persuade and educate segments of society that have consistently resisted the goals of the movement. Communication is essential and trade-book publishing is still one of the most effective means for getting the word out to thinking people. A strategy for scholars and teachers of women's studies to persuade publishers to pay attention to the needs and the potential profitability of the women's studies market might include the following tactics:

*Educate editors and publishers

When you deal with an editor regarding a publishing project be certain to define the significance of the project for future research and teaching; profile the market and discuss what the sale might be to institutions and libraries, to scholars working in the field, to students for course adoption, and to the audience of women readers. Support your argument with evidence of the demand for specific material by citing a review in *Signs* or *Women's Studies Quarterly* that describes a book that needs to be written or material that should be collected in an anthology or suggests a book that needs a paperback edition to be adopted in courses. Cite the comments of colleagues teaching in other schools who endorse a title for reprint or will assign a title in paperback. Encourage your colleagues to join in a lobbying effort by writing letters to an editor in support of a specific project—perhaps bringing back into print a lost nineteenth-century writer or issuing a paperback edition of a book.

*Organize and attend special sessions at MLA and NWSA

The little information editors do possess about the women's studies market comes from the reports of college marketing managers and college travelers and from their own occasional attendance at one of the major professional meetings where there is a strong division of feminists. Take advantage of these meetings to seek out and meet editors at the publishers' booths in the book exhibits; enlist their participation in seminars and special sessions in which scholars and teachers can discuss with editors publishing policies and programs for women's studies materials.

*Volunteer your time and service

Once you have established a working relationship with an editor, volunteer to act as a consultant to recommend projects worthy of publication or to read and evaluate manuscripts for the academic market. Suggest the names of scholars who would be appropriate to write introductions to out-of-print texts in order to bring them back into print.

If teachers and scholars in women's studies can establish collegial and collaborative relations with the editors of trade publishing houses and if scholars can produce books that perform well in the marketplace, then scholars and editors can more effectively argue for the more specialized work that might otherwise be lost without their joint sponsorship.

Notes

1. Unless otherwise specified, when I refer to the book business I mean trade book publishers who issue books in hardcover and paperback for the general reading public.
2. E. L. Doctorow, "Words into Rhinestones," *New York Times*, 19 March 1980, Sec. A, p. 22.
3. N. R. Kleinfield, "The Problems at Bantam Books," *New York Times Book Review*, 4 May 1980, p. 7.
4. N. R. Kleinfield, "A Troubled Time for Publishing," *New York Times*, 9 Oct. 1980, Sec. D, p. 6.
5. For an interesting view of the development of the paperback industry, see *At Random: The Reminiscences of Bennett Cerf* (New York: Random, 1977), pp. 195–206.
6. *B.P. Reports*, 23 June 1980, p. 9; 14 July 1980, p. 14.
7. Reprinted with permission from Maxwell J. Lillienstein, "Concentration and Other Threats to the Book Industry," *American Bookseller*, Oct. 1980, p. 23.
8. Martha King, "Who Reads in the United States?" *Coda: Poets & Writers Newsletter*, 7 (Sept.-Oct. 1979), 5–6.

Academic Writing
and Rejection

Emily Toth

Usually it's a form letter: "Thank you for sending us your article, _____ , for our journal. We find it is not suitable to our needs at this time, however, and we are herewith returning it to you." The would-be publishing scholar is left to wonder: What did I do wrong?

Most academic journals are overburdened with submissions; many have neither the time, the energy, nor the postage money to write personal rejection letters. Still, most journals reject badly written, badly presented, and inappropriate articles, and a scholarly writer can improve her chances for reaching print. There's some luck involved, and some chutzpah—but mostly getting published depends on writing well and having something to say.

When I was editor of *Regionalism and the Female Imagination* (formerly the *Kate Chopin Newsletter*) and consequently eager to publish feminist scholarship, I received numerous manuscripts that ignored the basic rules of academic writing. I was sent manuscripts with no footnotes, incomplete footnotes, or incorrect references; paste-up jobs with arrows running from part of one page to part of another page, so that I had to be a visual acrobat even to read the piece; dittoed submissions that I could barely make out in bright light; papers without self-addressed stamped envelopes; xeroxed papers (most journals prefer originals); and even papers without return addresses. Mostly I struggled through these anyway, but I became less and less inclined to do so. A writer who does not care how she presents her work suggests that she takes her writing less seriously than she should—and usually this attitude shows in the content.

Contrary to popular opinion, few articles are rejected for content alone. Sometimes, of course, the content is simply inappropriate for the journal: an article on Swift, for instance, would not belong in *Regionalism and the Female Imagination*. But an author can avoid rejection for content by studying the journal before she submits anything. She should scrutinize not only subject matter but also length, critical approach, and style (long-winded academic? terse and epigrammatic? cryptic?). She should check announcements of special issues and calls for papers: in *PMLA*'s Professional Notes and Comment, in *Concerns*, in the *Women's Studies Quarterly*, in the *Popular Culture Association Newsletter*, in fliers distributed at conventions and sent to departments. And she should share notices with her friends: why not an "old girls'" network?

Further, many journal editors welcome letters asking about length, approach, or style; briefly describing the article's subject and thesis; and (perhaps) including the writer's credentials for the undertaking. (I'm not swayed by a writer's credentials, but some editors seem to be.) A sample query letter:

Dear Professor Toth:

I have a twelve-page essay, "Style and Form in Kate Chopin's 'Ripe Figs,'" which I would like to send to *Regionalism and the Female Imagination* for possible publication. My article is essentially a formalist reading, taking into account similes, metaphors, sentence length, and syntax as keys to Chopin's stylistic success.

I did my dissertation at Louisiana State University on Chopin, Mary E. Wilkins Freeman, and Grace King and have published an essay on King in *Studies in Short Fiction*.

Please let me know if my article seems suitable for your publication.

Free-lance writers have always written query letters before sending their articles, and as an editor I found queries more useful—and easier to respond to—than completed manuscripts. I would, in fact, have told this writer that *Regionalism and the Female Imagination* would not be interested in seeing her article. Our journal—as we indicated in our fliers—focused on broader questions rather than on formalist readings of a single work. We wanted to rediscover forgotten writers, suggest critical approaches to regionalism, apply feminist critical questions to writings we knew—in short, this author's article would be both too narrow and too traditional for us. I could tell her so by return mail; reading her manuscript and circulating it among two other referees might take months.

A thorny issue: some journals may reject articles for feminist content, as I would reject purely formalist readings—but I cannot prove they do so. I do know that some journals—among them *MidAmerica,* the *University of Dayton Review,* and *Southern Studies*—would publish more articles on women writers if they received more.[1] The editors of *Chaucer Review, Seventeenth-Century News,* and *Journal of General Education*—all published in my department—are quite emphatic: they do not reject articles for unusual critical approaches.

Chaucer Review, for instance, has accepted two Jungian analyses of the Wife of Bath's Tale, though the editor himself, Robert W. Frank Jr., is hardly a Jungian ("I don't subscribe to half the things I publish"). As long as the article is useful to Chaucerians, he will print it. Harrison Meserole, editor of *Seventeenth-Century News,* confesses himself "stuffier" but adds that, since the seventeenth century is "multifarious," it would be hard to find any approach that's inappropriate. He has a particular fondness for wit and satire. Caroline D. Eckhardt, editor of the *Journal of General Education,* says her prejudices have more to do with style, organization, and documentation than with an article's approach but provides a caution valuable to feminist scholars: "If the approach is idiosyncratic, the writing had better be good."

Ultimately, as the South Atlantic Modern Language Association Women's Caucus study "72 Best Markets for New Scholars" reveals, poor writing (with its usual companion, dullness) is the major reason that manuscripts are rejected. All journal editors have received articles that are, quite simply, boring. Sometimes they rehash what's been said before: when I used to see that a writer had not checked what other scholars had done, I would reject her article, because she had not done her homework. Occasionally, of course, the subject itself would be trivial or uninteresting—but a good writer can illuminate almost anything, make us see her topic in a new light. Unfortunately, few academics are trained to become good writers.

Part of the fault lies with graduate school. Only one of my graduate school professors emphasized writing interesting prose; the others seemed to accept or even advise that seriousness, dullness, obscurity, and profundity were closely related. (One, in fact, suggested I was writing "high journalism": my prose was too clear.) All writers should, of course, write what "sells"—but what sells in graduate school is not usually what sells in scholarly publications.[2]

The problem with graduate school writing is that it's written without authority. The writer is, rightly, concerned with reading everything on a given subject, but she is not apt to create her own synthesis or her own new slant on the material. Graduate school papers tend to make tedious articles because they lack an individual voice. The writer seems to be a bibliographer rather than an authentic self shaping her material to prove her own thesis.

A writer need not use "I" to express herself; some journals, though fewer than one might suppose, still feel that "I" does not belong in scholarly writing. Rather, the writer's self should emerge through arrangement of her material. But many scholars do not know how to organize their material to prove a point—though organization is perhaps the easiest of all skills to learn and use.

The standard organization in an academic article involves five steps, as once outlined by Donald C. Stewart in *College English:*

1. statement of the problem
2. review of the relevant scholarship
3. statement of method in discussing the problem
4. analysis of evidence to support generalizations
5. conclusion.[3]

The pattern is easy to follow, and though Stewart suggests it is "a sterile and unimaginative paradigm," a parody of the scientific method, it is the pattern most journal editors seem to favor. (Again, a writer must write what "sells" in her market.)

The statement of the problem is the most important part: like the lead in a newspaper or magazine article, it must grab the reader. When I see a lead beginning "It is to be noted that recent scholarship has not accounted for either the prevalence of or the significance of . . ." I'm tipped off: turgid prose. I will usually slog my way through, out of dedication to duty, but my initial negative impression is almost always confirmed. Many journal editors will not even read an article that doesn't capture their interest in the first page or two. (Seventy percent of *Seventeenth-Century News* submissions are not sent on to a second reader.)

Yet it's surprisingly easy to write a good lead, and anyone who studies nonfiction prose can see the essential pattern. A good lead has a "hook," often a generalization about literature, life, or both. Even a cliché will do, as long as it's brief. A sentence or two later is the "twist": a sentence beginning with "But," "Yet," or a similar word and contrasting with the hook. The twist gets one or two supporting sentences. Finally, the sentence in the lead paragraph states the thesis, and summarizes the author's approach. An example:

> Recent poetry about abortion suggests the complexity of woman's dilemma. These poems do not reflect the casual attitude attributed to the twentieth-century woman who decides to reject the fetus. Rather, they show an emotional involvement recalling an earlier period, when childbirth teemed with terror, and death hovered close to life. Conscious of "the children you got that you did not get," the poets also link their works to a larger question: what is the relevance of children to the life of a woman?[4]

This kind of lead has its purest form in magazine writing. In academic writing, the lead paragraph is apt to be a bit longer. Sometimes the sentences are moved around a bit (as in this article), but the basic hook-twist-thesis organization remains. And the thesis, of course, is the most important organizing device in the entire paper.

Although literary-critics-in-training spend hours reading and writing about prose, they are rarely encouraged to see writing as a craft they too can develop. Rather, they learn to disparage composition and to disdain learning the composition techniques that will make their own writing clear and acceptable for publication. What most academic writing needs can be found in any freshman composition textbook: a topic sentence for each paragraph, followed by major and minor supports.

Such an organization seems cut-and-dried, and perhaps uncreative, but it makes all the difference. When I received a manuscript whose organization I could follow; whose thesis was developed successively, paragraph by paragraph, with transitions, through topic sentences and supports; whose conclusion flowed easily and naturally from the evidence put forth—I was grateful, even ecstatic. That article is rare indeed.

Equally rare is an article avoiding wordiness and jargon, the major sins of academese and dissertationese. Quotations, plot summaries, and footnotes abound; controversial terms, such as "irony," go undefined. Insecure writers cling to the passive voice, Latinate diction ("dichotomous actualization" rather than "double view"), and excessive qualifiers and apologetics. The respondents in "72 Best Markets" were sometimes scathing about the writing they received. *Virginia Quarterly Review* has rejected articles for "sloppy style, bad spelling, and academic gobbledygook"; *Southern Humanities Review* complained of "dull, stodgy, or pretentious development of argument"; and *Philological Quarterly* cited inadequate scholarship, "trivial or arcane subject ... pretentious or insipid style."[5]

As an editor, I did reject several articles simply for their bad style. I could not understand them, nor did I find trying to decipher them enjoyable. When I see such prose, my eyes glaze over, my heartbeat slows, and eventually my head sinks on my chest: I snore.

Some journals specialize in difficult prose, but most prefer theirs lucid. All would-be academic writers should invest in William Zinsser's *On Writing Well*, a how-to book with excellent suggestions for writing clearly, eschewing "clutter."[6] Zinsser emphasizes the ends of paragraphs: each paragraph should end with something important. These "thumps" keep the pace moving, even with the most scholarly of subjects. (I've tried to put a thump at the end of most paragraphs here. The reader should be able to "feel" what happens when I don't have a thump.)

Further, scholars who want to publish should read good writing: Carolyn G. Heilbrun's *Toward a Recognition of Androgyny,* Virginia Woolf's essays, Philip Young's *Three Bags Full* (esp. "The End of Compendium Reviewing," to see how even a compendium book review can be lively and witty, with an engaging "I" to guide us).[7] Read Edith Wharton, whose balanced sentences are superb models. Read the *New York Review of Books* and the *Massachusetts Review:* the timely literary articles in both begin with a "hook" and express the author's own voice and individuality.

Good markets, good models—what else can the fledgling scholar do? She should use the resources around her: the department bibliographer knows library materials; friends can give supportive criticism.[8] The would-be scholar should write to journals, offering to review books: many journals desperately need reviewers. She should write every day: keep a diary, write letters, or compose odes to the mail carrier. Anything to develop fluency and overcome the fear of the blank page.

Finally, she should trust herself and listen to her own voice. We all have an ear for style and an appreciation for content; if we didn't, we would not be literary people. A writer should not send out something she doesn't believe in or doesn't care about: her attitude will show in her writing. She should try to be aware of scholarly politics, which sometimes influence whether an article is selected for publication— and author-anonymous reviewing is a great aid to women scholars. But most of all, the fledgling scholar should find what moves or excites her in the writers or texts she's studying—and communicate that enthusiasm to her audience, directly and clearly. Then editors will rise up and call her blessed, tenure committees will smile, and the world of scholarship will be enriched.

Notes

1. I learned about *MidAmerica* through an announcement in *Regionalism and the Female Imagination*, 3 (Fall 1977 and Winter 1977–78), 122; the *University of Dayton Review* through "72 Best Markets for New Scholars," a SAMLA Women's Caucus survey directed by Martha E. Cook in 1977.

2. Everyone knows, I'm sure, someone whose graduate seminar paper was accepted by *PMLA*, but that person isn't the average scholar in training. Journal editors responding to a question about rejection (in "72 Best Markets for New Scholars") described seminar papers as generally unpublishable because of one or more common flaws: most frequently, narrowness, lack of originality, or poor writing.

3. Donald C. Stewart, "Rhetorical Malnutrition in Prelim Questions and Literary Criticism," *College English*, 39 (Oct. 1977), 160–68. R. B. McKerrow's wise and witty piece "Form and Matter in the Publication of Research," *PMLA*, 65 (April 1950), 3–8, labels the five parts
   1. The introduction
   2. The proposal
   3. The boost ("in which [the author] proceeds to magnify the importance of his discovery or argument and to explain what a revolution it will create in the views generally held on the whole period with which he is dealing. This is, as it were, a taste of sauce to stimulate the reader's appetite.")
   4. The demonstration
   5. The conclusion, or crow.

4. Irene Dash, "The Literature of Birth and Abortion," *Regionalism and the Female Imagination*, 3 (Spring 1977), 8, with slight revisions by E. Toth.

5. South Atlantic MLA Women's Caucus, ed. Martha E. Cook, "72 Best Markets for New Scholars," no pagination. Richard M. Dorson has a useful 30-item questionnaire "Academic Writing: Some Personal Tests," with pointed questions:
   * Do you use the passive voice without a subject?
   * Do you weigh the balance, the feel, the rhythm of your sentences?
   * Do you end sentences with weak words, like "it"?
   * Do you believe that to be readable is to be unscholarly?

   See Dorson's "The Scholar as Artist," *Chronicle of Higher Education*, 7 Nov. 1977, p. 40.

6. William Zinsser, *On Writing Well* (New York: Harper, 1976). See esp. chapters "Clutter" (pp. 13–17), "Style" (pp. 18–21), and "Words" (pp. 29–35).

7. Carolyn G. Heilbrun, *Toward a Recognition of Androgyny* (New York: Harper, 1973); Philip Young, *Three Bags Full* (New York: Harcourt, 1972), esp. pp. 30–54.

8. Several Chicago women have a "circle," meeting regularly to share papers and to provide critiques of one another's work. The SAMLA Women's Caucus heard an earlier draft of this paper, and my friend Susan Koppelman read and criticized it for me.

Additional Bibliography
for the Would-Be Publishing Scholar

Altick, Richard. *The Art of Literary Research.* New York: Norton, 1963, esp. pp. 181–202. Source of most of my bibliography.

Barzun, Jacques, and Henry F. Graff. *The Modern Researcher.* New York: Harcourt, 1957, pp. 229–87.

Carkeet, David. "How Critics Write and How Students Write," *College English,* 37 (Feb. 1976), 559–604.

Diamond, Arlyn. "Feminists Publishing." Women's Caucus for the Modern Languages Panel 2, MLA Convention, San Francisco, 27 Dec. 1975.

Douglas, Wallace W. "Souls among Masterpieces: The Solemn Style of Modern Critics," *American Scholar,* 23 (Winter 1953–54), 43–55.

Morison, Samuel Eliot. "History as a Literary Art," in *By Land and by Sea.* New York: Knopf, 1953, pp. 289–98.

Pell, William. "Facts of Scholarly Publishing." *PMLA,* 88 (1973), 639–70.

What's in a Name?

The Case for
Author-Anonymous
*Reviewing Policies**

Domna C. Stanton

"*Must* a name mean something?" asks Alice in *Through the Looking Glass.* "Of course it does," Humpty Dumpty replies, "my name means the shape I am."[1] In literature, as in life, almost all first names denote, by convention, the sex or biological "shape" of their possessor. Even more, a particular male or female name evokes arbitrary meanings that reflect and reveal the culture's ideology. In a recent study conducted at Pennsylvania State University and the Ohio State University, psychologists Barbara Buchanan and James Robinson found a remarkable consensus of opinion among a thousand college students who were asked to evaluate first names; for example, they endorsed "Michael" and "Wendy" as "extremely masculine" and "quite feminine," respectively, while expressing strong doubts about "Percival's" masculinity and "Alfreda's" femininity.[2] This devaluation of a man's name suggesting a certain prissiness and delicacy[3] or of a woman's name containing a visibly masculine root (Alfred) points to the continuing hold of traditional stereotypes of masculinity and femininity on college students, a group generally believed to articulate society's more liberal views. Like the labels on bathroom doors, "masculine" and "feminine" still define two inviolable categories that comprise a network of binary oppositions. Their connotations, like those of the more "neutral" terms "female" and "male," are a product of phallocentric thinking that predicates negating women in order to validate men. For instance, in a well-known study undertaken by I. Broverman, D. Broverman, and others, social workers, psychologists, and psychiatrists (46 men and 33 women) were divided in three groups and asked to select from 122 bipolar terms those that described "a healthy, mature, socially competent a) adult, sex unspecified, b) a man or c) a woman." The results showed that these accredited definers of health and sociability strongly correlated the traits for desirable male and desirable adult behavior but characterized the "healthy female" as "more submissive, less independent, less adventurous, more easily influenced, less aggressive . . . more emotional . . . less objective, and disliking math and science."[4]

Such findings underscore the deep-seated discrimination that women confront in the work place even from the more enlightened and educated members of society. By implication, having a female name and "shape" suffices to create the assumption that women's work will be "less independent, adventurous, objective and scientific" than men's; in other words, that it will be second-rate. As studies by Philip Goldberg have confirmed, the mere presence of a gynonym (Joan T. McKay) rather than an andronym (John T. McKay)—indeed, the minute but gender-identifying change of a single letter—produced in eighty-one percent of the cases tested a marked difference in the evaluation of identical texts, to the serious disadvantage of the female author.[5] Replicated for both the written and the visual arts by researchers such as Bem and Bem,[6] these studies document the existence of a stereotypic subtext that determines judgments first presented and then valorized by our society as objective. When these judgments are made by powerful members of a profession, they have a crucial impact on women's careers.

In a diachronic perspective, the same subtextual stereotypes of femaleness have determined the critical reputations of women's writing. As feminist scholars have repeatedly shown during the last decade, men have used the sex of the author to denigrate the text by transferring to the writing itself dominant stereotypes of femininity. In Mary Ellman's words:

> The discussion of women's books by men will arrive punctually at the point of preoccupation, which is the fact of femininity. Books by women are treated as though they themselves were women, and criticism embarks, at its happiest, upon an intellectual measuring of busts and hips.[7]

A case in point is Louis Kronenberger's estimation of Virginia Woolf's work: "The writers who are most downright and masculine, and central in their approach to life—a Fielding or a Balzac, she for the most part left untouched. . . . Her own approach was at once more subterranean and aerial and invincibly, almost defiantly, feminine." More recently, Louis Auchincloss could dismiss contemporary women novelists with this sexist remark: "It is difficult to avoid the strident note, the shrill cry."[8] Most of us will smile with a gleam of superiority at such blatant phallic criticism and proclaim ourselves incapable of such fallacies. But in so doing we deny the truth that human beings are incapable of making fully objective judgments, that we are all carriers of society's prejudices. To accept our complicity in the dominant ideology is only a first step, however. The critical question is whether we will consciously institutionalize practices to ensure that our judgments of others' merits are as uncorrupted as possible by our unconscious biases. It is in this context that the case for author-anonymous reviewing policies in publishing needs to be made.

Author-anonymous reviewing refers to the editorial practice of withholding the identity of the author from those who evaluate a manuscript submitted for publication. A term that has fewer negative connotations than "blind refereeing," as the policy has also been called, author-anonymous reviewing has provoked considerable controversy in the humanities in recent years,[9] most especially in literature, where the practice is the exception rather than the rule. Statements made by the editors of thirty-eight scholarly journals in 1977 indicate that only six used an author-anonymous reviewing policy: *General Linguistics, Italian Quarterly,* the *Journal of Esthetics and Art Criticism,* the *Journal of Asian Studies, SIGNS: Journal of Women in Culture and Society,* and *Victorian Studies.*[10] Significantly, 2 of these 6 journals (or 33%) were edited by women (Catharine R. Stimpson of *SIGNS* and Martha Vicinus of *Victorian Studies*), as compared to a total of 3 women editors in the group of 38 (or 8%). Since then *German Quarterly* adopted the policy under its new editor, Ruth Angress, and *PMLA* instituted the practice, in January, 1980, after a three-year debate initiated by the Modern Language Association's Commission on the Status of Women.

"As a general rule, the harder the science the greater [the] ease with which blind reviewing is accepted," William D. Schaefer, the former executive director of the MLA, has written. "As you move toward literature, the resistance to blind reviewing becomes more intense. It has to do with the degree of allowance for facts to speak for themselves. The more self in the article, the greater the difficulty for anonymous review."[11] Schaefer's notion of personal traces in literary but not in scientific scholarship requires some qualification and comment about all three branches of knowledge. Unlike literature in particular and the humanities in general, the social sciences have accepted author-anonymous reviewing as the norm in scholarly journals since the 1940s. Indeed, the MLA's survey of the forty-three constituent soci-

eties of the American Council of Learned Societies in 1977 revealed
that the five largest associations with this policy were all in the social
sciences—anthropologists, economists, political scientists, psychologists, and sociologists. Although the precise reasons for the disparity in
the editorial practices of the humanities and the social sciences are not
clear, Jonathan Cole, a sociologist, speculates that social scientists are
intrinsically

> concerned with the influence of people's personal characteristics
> and values in decision-making. Consequently, social scientists were
> aware earlier on that the particular characteristics of producers and
> consumers of knowledge could influence the evaluation and selec-
> tion of manuscripts for publication.[12]

When we turn to the "harder sciences," as Schaefer terms them, we
do not find a widespread acceptance of author-anonymous reviewing.
According to Harriet Zuckerman, a sociologist who surveyed some one
hundred scientific journals in the early 1970s, practice varies greatly,
but scientists generally claim that the policy cannot be put into effect
in specialized fields where researchers all know one another's work,
methodology, and style.[13] Gisella Pollock, an editor involved with the
publications of the American Society of Microbiologists, explains: "Perhaps it is possible to keep the author anonymous in some other disciplines. But in microbiology the areas of research are so defined that
there is only a limited number of people working in each area" (Maeroff, p. 4). Moreover, as Jonathan Cole argues, "the myth of objectivity
is particularly tenacious in scientific circles," a myth to which Irwin
Neter, who served as editor of *Infection and Immunity* for ten years,
strongly subscribes: "In my opinion, the vast, vast majority of scientists
who review scientific papers such as those submitted to my journal are
objective and will not be influenced by an author's name or institutional affiliation" (Maeroff, p. 4). And yet, in Cole's view, some scientists
are beginning "to realize that a good deal of their activities are condi-
tioned by personal values and tastes and individual characteristics"; he
notes that in the last decade most of the pressure on scientists to alter
their views on objectivity and their policies on publication have come
from women's organizations.

At the same time, there is one salient fact that renders author-anonymous reviewing less than critical in scientific journals: by Zuckerman's computations, 8 or 9 out of every 10 articles submitted are
actually published. If anything, adds Cole, editors worry about rejecting studies that may turn out to be significant; the predominant editorial function "is not one of exclusion, as in the humanities, but of
inclusion." When one considers, by comparison, that in the period
1973–77 only 6.1% of the 2,500 articles submitted to *PMLA* were ac-

cepted for publication,[14] then the "intense resistance" to author-anonymous reviewing in literary scholarship, which Schaefer rightly recognizes, becomes easier to understand. This resistance surely has little to do with the degree of "self" in scholarly writing, as Schaefer maintains, since the speaking "I," or subject of enunciation, constitutes a textual persona and not an actual person; in Wayne Booth's terms, it is the implied rather than the real author.[15] Nor, after all, can we assume a greater degree of personal involvement or of narcissism among scholars in literature than in other academic disciplines. In the absence of existing studies, we may conjecture, however, that behind the intense resistance of senior literary scholars and editors, who are, almost all, white males, lies a fear of exclusion, of being denied the relatively easy access to one another's journals that they now possess, of being reduced to the level of unknown assistant professors and subjected to the same scrutiny. Author-anonymous reviewing may well pose the threat of losing one of the few perquisites and privileges that a senior professor of literature enjoys in our society. A symbolic castration, it evokes the possibility of being robbed of a powerful weapon that senior scholars secretly believe is rightfully theirs.[16]

The historical moment at which author-anonymous reviewing found its activist proponents among young literary scholars is surely not accidental. The desire to institutionalize egalitarian practices in publishing derives from the same liberal impulse of the 1960s that produced in the academy some changes in the curriculum (black and women's studies, e.g.) and in admission and hiring policies (affirmative action aimed at increasing the percentage of women and minority students and faculty). As the economic crisis of the 1970s has led to ever fiercer competition for a diminishing number of jobs, enormous pressures have been put on young humanists to publish within five years after completion of the doctorate an amount that would have represented a respected scholar's lifework only a generation ago. In this climate, it is hardly surprising that young academics, especially females, whose aspirations have been raised by the women's movement, should press for policies that signal their work will be judged on its intrinsic merits and not on irrelevant factors of gender. Of course, author-anonymous reviewing can do more than combat prejudice against femaleness (as denoted by a name). It can protect those whose names are unknown from discrimination that favors the well-known; it can also eliminate unconscious bias against those who are unemployed or employed at black, community, or women's colleges, which are deemed unprestigious in comparison to research universities with national reputations. In a word, then, author-anonymous reviewing may provide the relatively powerless in the academy with more equal access to the means of scholarly production and thus a chance not only to improve their professional status but also, in these desperate times, to survive in the academy.[17] Yet, since the second sex is concentrated in the lower academic ranks at less prestigious institutions and with lower salaries than men receive, author-anonymous reviewing has greater import for women than for men, even minority men, who do not bear the additional burden of sexism. In the 1970s, when a conservative backlash largely stifled liberal political thought and praxis, with the notable exception of the women's movement, it was academic feminists who actively fought for the adoption of author-anonymous reviewing policies in the humanities against "intense resistance" from those who had the power to determine who speaks and who remains silent, who publishes and who perishes.[18]

The arguments that senior scholars and editors of literary journals advance in opposition to author-anonymous reviewing tend to follow familiar lines.[19] The first is the humanistic argument, which views "anonymity as antihumane as any notion can be" and the policy as secretive, inimical to openness, destructive of the ideal community of scholars.[20] Obviously it could be argued that the journal that tries to avoid bias through such procedures is more "open" than one that rejects them, provided we understand "open" to mean a journal whose pages are not reserved for a preselected few. The more fundamental argument for the humanity of author-anonymous reviewing has been voiced by Lee C. R. Baker:

> the equation of humanism with a name on a manuscript is just as mechanical . . . as the reductive and tired old bias against the sciences in general. . . . To keep the names of the authors from the reviewer does not mean that the essays are products from a computer, disconnected from the lives of their makers. One may take an impersonal view of an article and yet not forget the humanity of the author. Humanism is manifest in the fairness with which the reviewer explores, understands, and sympathizes with an author's efforts to explain a point of view. . . . Anonymous review, insofar as it assures the unbiased consideration of articles, will not damage the community of scholars. It will, on the contrary, help to ensure the community's trust in the fairness of the editorial procedures of the organization that claims to be its representative. (*MLA Newsletter,* Fall 1978, p. 5)

Another "humanistic" argument against author-anonymous reviewing is that the practice would destroy dialogue between authors and referees because the quality of evaluative reports would decline. Flippancy, even brutality, it is claimed, would replace lengthy and substantive commentary. This argument assumes that scholars are essentially incapable of serious and respectful attention to the work of their peers, indeed, that only an author's name can force them to be professionally responsible. Nevertheless, this criticism, which is invariably made by those who have never used the policy, is not validated by my own six-year experience as the associate editor of *SIGNS*, where reports continued to be substantial and lengthy. Their quality confirmed the existence of a genuine community of scholars interested in evaluating one another's ideas and not the name (or rank or institution) of the author. Moreover, those who raise the banner of quality reports often admit, like old-fashioned biographical critics, that they are incapable of writing a textual critique without knowing the author's background. "It would be hard for me to know what to say in way of review if I were ignorant about the writer to whom ultimately I am speaking," confessed Daniel Silvia, although he couched this inability beneath such sentiments as the value of dialogue and a common cause (*MLA Newsletter*, Fall 1978, p. 4). In point of fact, a process whereby the author is known to the reviewer but the reviewer unknown to the author constitutes monologue, not dialogue. It is a one-way process and, by and large, a one-time process.

Leaving the reviewing process aside, opponents also maintain that author-identification policies allow editors to promote the work of young scholars. Repeatedly, editors aver paternalistically that they bend over backwards to give young scholars a chance. "If there has been any kind of bias," Schaefer, the former editor of *PMLA*, has stated, "it has been in favor of the younger, unknown person" (Herbert, p. 6). Judging from *PMLA*'s own published statistics, however, this bending has not been particularly strenuous. In the period 1973–77, assistant professors accounted for 38.7% of all submissions and 34.4% of all acceptances; full professors for 16.3% of submissions and 27.8% of acceptances.[21] And when we add gender to these statistics, we find that male full professors have the highest acceptance rate (11.1%), whereas female full professors have an acceptance rate of only 4.4%; in Schaefer's own words, "no similar correlation exists [for women] between high rank and high percentage of acceptances." Even in the lower ranks, the rates of acceptance for females, notes Schaefer, are visibly lower than those for males. If we reject a priori the notion that women produce scholarship inferior to that of men, then we must conclude that prejudice plays a decisive role in such statistics. It should be understood, moreover, that proponents of author-anonymous reviewing do not advocate this purported "bending over backwards" for female or younger scholars (which is perniciously called "reverse discrimination"). The publication of "inferior" scholarship does not serve the interests of women (or the powerless); on the contrary, it perpetuates their second-class status by providing examples of their second-rate work. All texts should be accepted on the basis of the same criteria, which should be implemented through the most impartial procedures we can devise. Paternalism, and I use the word advisedly, should have no place in publishing.

Admittedly, the celebrated scholar does present certain problems for author-anonymous reviewing. It could be argued that what Roman Jakobson, Frances Yates, Wayne Booth, and Julia Kristeva say will be useful to a large number of scholars and thus that their identities should be known to the reviewer. Or, to cite the name that invariably comes up in this connection: "If Northrop Frye writes an article attacking archetypal criticism, what he says is, ipso facto, important," Stanley Fish has written (Herbert, p. 5). This argument ignores the possibility that journals with author-anonymous reviewing practices can still commission articles or that occasionally a celebrated scholar, whose identity cannot be concealed, may be exempted from an inevitably ritualistic refereeing process. And yet, there is a real danger that the number of these rare individuals will be increased to the point of creating a new two-class system, that the most insignificant work of the celebrated will be treated as oracular or, as we are witnessing ever more frequently today, that journals will publish nothing but commissioned articles. More important, however, is the fundamental speciousness of an argument that cites the exception to condemn egalitarian practices for the many, a logic that would be disastrous if applied to the law of any civilized society. In an answer to Fish's argument, Catharine R. Stimpson comments: "Obviously, there will be cases where anonymity is impossible. Frye would be identified by internal evidence in any case, but most people do not fall into this special class" (Herbert, p. 6).

Stimpson's statement is an implicit answer to yet another argument advanced against author-anonymous reviewing: the difficulties of implementing the procedure and of ensuring anonymity. Editors who rely on this policy, however, usually stress its efficiency and facility. According to Martha Vicinus of *Victorian Studies,* which adopted the practice over six years ago, "anonymity is maintained 85–90% of the time with little or no difficulty."[22] That the system may occasionally break down is, of course, no reason to reject the practice; it simply suggests the need for vigilance to guarantee anonymity wherever possible. Each journal must establish the degree of anonymity that can reasonably be maintained, partly determined by the degree of specialization of the field and the size of the journal's staff. For small journals, the name of the author can surely be kept from referees but not from the editor, who should then rely almost exclusively on reader evaluations in reaching a decision. For larger journals with a staff that can code submissions, it is easy to maintain anonymity until an article is accepted or rejected.

As a last resort, opponents of author-anonymous reviewing argue that instances of bias are grossly exaggerated. In the absence of existing studies that compare results before and after adoption of these procedures, the basis for such a statement is clearly subjective. In fact, the one case that has been documented suggests radically different facts. In the annual proceedings of the American Philological Association, the Committee on the Status of Women and of Minority Groups reported that the percentage of papers written by women and accepted for presentation at the association's annual convention almost *tripled* (from 6.7% to 19.5%) within two years after author-anonymous reviewing had been put into practice, whereas during the same period journals in the field not using this policy showed, if anything, a slight decrease in the number of published articles by women.[23] As classicist Mary Lefkowitz has said, the results were even more dramatic than activists had anticipated (Herbert, p. 4). Indeed, these findings, which the MLA's Commission on the Status of Women used in actively promoting author-anonymous procedures, helped convince the Executive Council to adopt them for *PMLA* with the proviso that a study evaluate the results after three years.[24]

Although the results may not reveal dramatic differences in rates of acceptance for articles by women, the unknown, the unemployed, and others, I still argue that the policy should be maintained. Even more, author-anonymous reviewing should be instituted in all academic journals and extended to include the evaluation of papers for academic congresses, of grant applications, and of book-length manuscripts. These procedures, like laws in our society, are important signs that we subscribe to egalitarianism both in theory and in practice. They bespeak the *effort* to ensure a fair and impartial judgment of our colleagues—perhaps the most that imperfect beings can hope for in an imperfect world. They declare our commitment to reason and humanism over and against the irrational and dehumanizing impulses that we all possess and that a mere name can still catalyze. To endorse these procedures is to say with Robert Lowell:

> I do not fear to follow out the truth
> Albeit along the precipice's edge.
> Let us speak plain; there is more force in names
> Than most men dream of; and a lie may keep
> Its throne a whole age longer, if it skulk
> Behind the shield of some fair-seeming myth.[25]

The institution of author-anonymous reviewing in all forms and modes of publishing constitutes a specific means for combating prejudices against women and the powerless that "skulk / Behind the shield" of such "fair-seeming" myths as "the objective judgments of a communi-

ty of scholars." More broadly, the policy is founded on the incontest-
able premise that the decisions determining who speaks and who
remains silent in institutional and professional contexts involve a dia-
lectic of power and thus the ideology of the culture. That women's
committees and commissions in associations such as the APA or the
MLA have actively fought for and achieved the institutionalization of
author-anonymous reviewing can serve as a signal to others that
change can be effected and that the status of the relatively powerless
can be ameliorated.

Some observers may interpret the efforts of female scholars to establish author-anonymous procedures as a paradoxical valorization and
perpetuation of the anonymity imposed on women authors throughout
the centuries. As Virginia Woolf wrote in *A Room of One's Own*, "I
would venture to say that Anon, who wrote so many poems without
signing them, was often a woman."[26] But author-anonymous reviewing
promotes a different mode of anonymity, one that functions only at
the beginning of a process and that affirms the inscription of the female name in the end. Instead of indulging in paradoxes, we must face
the realistic fact that, until women "hold up half the sky," anonymity
represents a positive alternative to the negative meanings still evoked
by a female name; it is a necessary albeit artificial measure for guaran-
teeing women the inalienable right to speak and thus to be. If we believe in the power of words, then it is not altogether idle to imagine
that the accumulated force of women's texts can help shake the phallo-
cratic edifices of "masculine" and "feminine" on which the culture
rests and, who knows, even change our vision of the existing sky.

Notes

*I want to thank Joan E. Hartman and Ellen Messer-Davidow for their valuable comments and suggestions on the first draft of this text. An abbreviated version of the final draft appeared in *Change* (May 1981, pp. 8–11).

1. Lewis Carroll, *Through the Looking Glass, the Annotated Alice,* ed. Martin Gardner (New York: Bramball, 1970), p. 63.
2. This study was reported in Mary G. Marcus, "The Power of a Name," *Psychology Today,* Oct. 1976, pp. 75–76.
3. I am intentionally not evoking the characteristics of the medieval Parsifal, with whom the average college student would probably not be familiar.
4. Inge K. Broverman, Donald M. Broverman, Frank E. Carlson, Paul S. Rosenkrantz, and Susan R. Vogel, "Sex-Role Stereotypes and Clinical Judgments of Mental Health," *Journal of Consulting and Clinical Psychology,* 34, No. 1 (1970), 1–7. For a recent analysis of the problem of stereotypes, see Rhoda K. Unger, *Female and Male: Sex and Gender* (New York: Harper, 1979).
5. Philip A. Goldberg, "Are Women Prejudiced against Other Women?" *Trans-Action,* No. 5 (1968), pp. 28–30.
6. Sandra L. Bem and Daryl J. Bem, "On Liberating the Female Student," *School of Psychology Digest,* 2, No. 3 (1973), 10–18.
7. Mary Ellman, *Thinking about Women* (New York: Harcourt, 1970), p. 29.
8. Louis Kronenberger, *The Republic of Letters* (New York: Knopf, 1955), p. 249; Louis Auchincloss, *Pioneers and Caretakers: A Study of Nine American Novelists* (Minneapolis: Univ. of Minnesota Press, 1965), p. 4.
9. See Gene I. Maeroff, "Journals' Problem: What to Publish," *New York Times,* 14 Aug. 1979, Sec. C, p. 1, col. 5; p. 4, cols. 5–6; further references to this article appear in the text.
10. This information comes from an unpublished study undertaken by the executive director of the MLA at the request of the Executive Council. Unfortunately, no complete study has ever been made to determine which journals of language and literature do use author-anonymous reviewing procedures. It is disappointing that the recently published *MLA Directory of Periodicals: A Guide to Journals and Series in Languages and Literatures, 1978–1979* (comp. Eileen M. Mackesy, Karen Mateyak, and Diane Siegel, with the assistance of the *MLA Bibliography* staff), which polled 2,877 journals and series, did not solicit this information from editors, along with the other questions asked pertaining to editorial practices.
11. Quoted in Wray C. Herbert, "Blind Reviewing, Hotly Debated, Taking Hold in Humanities Journals," *Humanities Report,* 2, No. 4 (1980), 5. Further references to this article appear in the text.
12. Personal communication with Jonathan Cole, professor of sociology at Columbia University; all other references to Cole in this article are taken from this source.
13. Personal communication with Harriet Zuckerman, professor of sociology, Columbia University; all other references to Zuckerman in this article are taken from this source.

14. William D. Schaefer "*PMLA* Profile—1," *MLA Newsletter*, Oct. 1977, p. 3.
15. See Wayne Booth, *The Rhetoric of Fiction* (Chicago: Univ. of Chicago Press, 1961), pp. 211–21 and throughout. Of course, some writers beg the "I" and use the royal "we," a term that assumes the existence of a community with identical educational, professional, social, sexual, or racial affiliations and values.
16. I mean to suggest not a pathology unique to senior literary scholars but, rather, a generalized mentality in the academic world (and perhaps in all institutions) that is dramatized through their specific situation. It represents the global conflict between the haves and the have-nots.
17. Clearly, however, author-anonymous reviewing procedures cannot remedy bias against certain "deviant" subjects and methodologies. In most instances, the reader who considers women's studies unscholarly or frivolous, for example, will evaluate a related article negatively. The reader or referee who holds such a priori views and who is usually ignorant of critical contexts and developments in the field should—but rarely does—recommend that an article would be more accurately evaluated by a specialist in Women's Studies.
18. As Louise Bernikow has said: "Which works have become part of the 'canon' of literature, read, thought about, discussed, and which have disappeared, depends ... on the process of selection and the power to select along the way. Such power, in England and America, has always belonged to white men" (*The World Split Open: Four Generations of Women Poets in England and America, 1552–1950.* [New York: Random, 1974], p. 3).
19. The following résumé of arguments against author-anonymous reviewing is largely taken from the pages of the *MLA Newsletter*, in which William D. Schaefer first presented his case against the practice (Summer 1978, pp. 4–6) and then published letters pro and con elicited by his article (Fall 1978, pp. 4–6).
20. *MLA Newsletter* (Fall 1978), p. 4. In a somewhat far-fetched analogy, Schaefer declared: "To me, anonymous review would be like asking all of us to wear masks and disguise our voices when we speak at meetings at the MLA Convention" (Summer 1978, p. 6).
21. "*PMLA* Profile—3," *MLA Newsletter*, Spring 1978, p. 3. In this light, it is hard to accept the statement of Jackson Cope, founder of *Studies in English Literature*, that "90% of what is published is written by young scholars who are in fact, if not by choice, anonymous" (quoted in Herbert, p. 6). This idea is somewhat analogous to the claim, contrary to all statistical evidence, that women and blacks are getting all the jobs in our society.
22. Personal communication with Martha Vicinus.
23. Jane M. Snyder et al., "Report on the Committee on the Status of Women and of Minority Groups," *Proceedings of the American Philolological Association*, 114 (1976), 17–22. Martha Vicinus confirms that the editorial staff of *Victorian Studies* did find cases of bias. She instituted author-anonymous reviewing when she realized that articles were being returned with the comment, "I can't imagine this man writing anything bad; you should publish it."
24. In this effort, I do not want to overlook the role that the Graduate Stu-

dents' Caucus (another association of the powerless) played in introducing the subject for discussion on the floor of the Delegate Assembly in 1977. The positive "sense of the meeting" that resulted from this discussion led the Executive Council in May 1978 to request a vote on the issue from the Delegate Assembly at the Assembly's December 1978 meeting. The overwhelming approval of the policy by this body facilitated the adoption of author-anonymous reviewing for *PMLA* at a moment when almost half of the Executive Council was composed of women, and the new Executive Director, Joel Conarroe, had taken office. The degree of personal involvement that author-anonymous policies generated within the MLA may be gauged by one remark made by Schaefer: "As soon as I turned my back, the MLA passed the policy" (Herbert, p. 5).

25. Robert Lowell, "A Glance behind the Curtain."
26. Virginia Woolf, *A Room of One's Own* (New York: Harcourt, 1957), p. 51.

Making Choices

Can Two Small-Town Feminists Publish with a Big-City Trade House and Remain Pure?

Susan Griffin and J. J. Wilson

Susan Griffin and J. J. Wilson got together to tape the following (considerably abridged) conversation on the policies of publishing. They were asked to focus on editor-author relations, based on their own experiences with one of the large trade houses. J. J. has written with Karen Petersen a paperback book on women artists, *Women Artists: Recognition & Reappraisal,* with accompanying slide sets published by Harper and Row. Susan has published a collection of poetry, *Like the Iris of an Eye,* with Harper and Row, as well as *Woman and Nature: The Roaring inside Her* and *Rape: The Power of Consciousness.* She has also published with women's presses: *Dear Sky* and *The Sink* (Shameless Hussy Press); *Voices* (Feminist Press); *Letter* (Effie's Press); *Let Then Be Said* (MaMa Press). The resulting "duologue" explores informally some of the issues of power and identification in work relations, issues that these two were concerned with and that may be crucial to the next decade of the women's movement.

S: Well, my *reason* for contracting with Harper & Row was economic—I had to have an advance for us to live on—but I do not deny that there is some part of me that felt exonerated for the eighteen or so years of writing I'd done because finally I was being presented by a "real publisher." Recognition by the father ... sure, that is an attitude I have to face in myself, and part of fighting it is to admit you've got it.

J: Well, I have to admit that when I held your book of poems from Harper's in my hands for the first time, tears just leapt from my eyes, and I showed it to everyone, as if that sort of endorsement would give us all permission to take women's writing seriously. Sounds silly now, but it meant something to me and means something to lots of potential readers.

S: Yes, and I'm very conscious of that. Those of us who are consciously political feminists, who write for political reasons, have to realize that we can't abandon certain conventional—not forms so much as forums—to reach women who still have patriarchal ears and will not hear us unless we're broadcast on that wave length. But I think there's a more complicated way of looking at the satisfaction I got. It was like winning a fierce, bitter battle that had been waged over the years, that I was certainly not fighting alone, and that I could never have won alone. After all, there was no way that Harper and Row would have ever published my poetry without a feminist movement and without the small women's presses. And it is essential that we keep these presses alive, which is like saying we must keep our culture alive. But we also need to go beyond the boundaries of that culture.

J: For my coauthor, Karen, and me, it was almost the point of our book that it be published by one of the big publishing houses, because it is a challenge to the very textbooks they put out, art history in our case, which seem almost to conspire to keep knowledge of women's work out of the educational system. Our book looks like a regular art history book, only these deeds were done by women, *dux femina facti,* as it says in the *Aeneid.* This cover, this disguise, this point would have been lost, I think, if we had come out only in an impassioned pamphlet or in a letter to the publishers about bias in their texts.

Also, and incidentally, at that time we did not know of any women's press that could have handled the technology of putting together a book that had over three hundred illustrations and that could sell at the low price of $5.95. Then there was the opportunity for a tie-in with Harper and Row's audiovisual department, which resulted in color slides being distributed, also economically, to schools and colleges, the market we aimed at from the beginning of the women artists project. Furthermore, as you said, Susan, the advance was essential, to pay the reproduction fees, postage costs, Karen's keep, and child care, which we insisted be a budget item, as a point both of principle and of necessity.

Oh, I can interpolate a whole lot of good practical and political reasons why we should have done the book with Harper and Row, whereas the actual decision was unconscious, happened very quickly. Molly Willcox, a scout for Harper at that time, heard our slide lecture and saw the book potential in it. We went on because our intuitions told us it was okay. And in fact it was okay, a positive experience. But it could have gone sour, and I don't recommend that sort of sleepwalking to other people. We were lucky in our production team, all women, and in our editor, Hugh van Dusen, who never censored us, even by implication, in content or in style.

S: Yes, I think the editor you are working with is so important; there can be a real *tsuris*—heartache, headache, misery—you can go through if you don't have a sympathetic editor. The ideas that I am dealing with in this new book on women and nature challenge the most basic patriarchal and Christian assumptions, the fabric of our thought. And I'm writing in a form that most people would call irrational, a totally associative poetic form, and I am making those kinds of links that aren't really rational because this is the point: I am positing that the history of "rational" thought has its own irrational bias. Initially I would wake up at night in a cold sweat of terror, thinking, oh my god I really should have twenty years of scientific training before I try to question the very history and assumptions of science. . . .

J: Catch 22.

S: Catch 22, of course, because if I'd had that kind of training, I couldn't be asking these questions. But I do know how to do vigorous research, and the work I was doing was served by my fear of the judgment of the Fathers as manifested by Harper and Row, because I was thorough and careful and accumulated massive documentation for my intuitions. Yet, ironically, Harper and Row was never actually critical in this regard—which is good, because in the long run, I feel, and am beginning to know, that to work in any way from fear is a waste.

My editor, Fran McCullough, gives me just the kind of support I need. I feel very comfortable working with her. For instance, when I was having trouble putting the final draft of the book together so that it would flow, Fran suggested I write a table of contents, a descriptive one such as they did in the eighteenth century, and this suggestion turned out to be marvelously helpful. Fran is a brilliant woman and the kind of editor you can go to and say, "I have a problem," secure in the knowledge that she will not use that vulnerability to try to take control of the manuscript.

J: Yes, we felt that too, that in the end our decision would be respected. And some women's presses, particularly if they didn't feel too secure, might have resisted certain turns of phrase and certain ideas we were pushing. At Harper and Row there is a kind of compact, like the autonomy-in-the-classroom compact; among all the compromises they have had to make, they still believe in the author as last authority, and they stick to that belief.

S: We have both been lucky, I think, because without that total trust, all sorts of uncertainties can creep in. *Ramparts* magazine, when

I published an article on rape in 1971, wanted a less personal tone. I felt the tone was essential to the theme, that we could no longer separate ourselves from the events under discussion, but it was an idea that I only had hold of lightly, and I could have been easily deflected. My advice would be, whatever the other issues of advances, distribution, and so on, you must consider the editor you will be working with. Don't ever overestimate your own strength in dealing with a personality, policies, and politics together.

J: There can be a kind of boomerang effect in working with a women's press. At least if you are working with a trade house, you can see the editor as your advocate and that's a good feeling, but you know all along that the trade house is the enemy. You keep alert to that, and you're in fighting trim all the time. Some people I know who have worked with women's presses have overidentified and, before they knew it, the women's press people were almost writing for the author the book they would like to be writing. The editor and author can lose that sense of their different roles, and then later, when the editor has to reemerge as publisher and when the authors have to recognize their position, there can be a sense of betrayal or of muddle at least.

S: This is one thing I've learned from working with "the boys": a recognition of ethical responsibilities on both sides comes from the understanding on both sides that you're in a potentially adversary position. I mean, I'm serious about feminism being able to establish and run the world, you know, and we do have to understand that there also are intrinsic conflicts that don't have anything to do with male and female or patriarchal and matriarchal. There are real power conflicts, and I think that a publisher and a writer are in a power conflict to begin with, and therefore a standard of ethics of behavior has to be set up. And I have a feeling that within the patriarchal publishing world it was often the women who forged, through organizations such as the Author's Guild, the means to protect the vulnerable individual artist from the institution's weight. And there is a weight that can be felt even when your political interests are not set in opposition, when a women's press says, for instance, "our collective has made this decision." Well, there you are, the writer, and what can you say? Well, my collective has made one too, I mean, myself, me, and I.

J: The pencil and the eraser, yeah.

S: But you know, they can talk to you, reason and argue with you, and you cannot talk with them because they are a collective.

J: They will have to refine their collective to make sure that they don't tyrannize the individual.

S: Yes, but we will always need organizations like the one we are founding now, the Feminist Writer's Guild, where any member of the guild can function as an advocate for another member.[1] The guild will

have policies and act as a collective too. It is a structure set up to balance the power that is there, though women are too often afraid to admit that it is there. We need structures to protect our rights of free
expression.

We've been socialized to think in the short term, because if a woman thought of her life in long term she wouldn't live it the way she's
supposed to. It's painful for anybody in a state of servitude to think in
any way other than from day to day, but in fact when you're doing
something as complicated as liberating and transforming an entire society, you've got to pace yourself and think about the long term.
There's a process going on, and at one point you can say it is right to
publish with a trade press, and at a different point it may not be right.
I dislike thinking of this question or any question in terms of an absolute and unchanging moral code.

J: Yes, for one thing the big trade presses are themselves changing,
becoming multicorporate outfits under the pressure of an overblown
capitalism that requires so much money to support itself that they will
soon topple over like . . .

S: It's a tautological construction.

J: Oh good, I don't know what that means.

S: I just made it up!

J: Well, I see what it could mean—that they are soon going to topple over like dinosaurs and become obsolete. And then the need for
the smaller presses, which will no longer be small presses, will be clear,
and our whole discussion here unnecessary. But at this point, in the
seventies, it seems that there are still more trade-offs than losses and
that certain books would not even come into being if it were not for
the trade presses.

S: Yes, for instance, the impact that *Sexual Politics* had, which I
think is inestimable. You know, that was a historical event in publication, and at that point the women's presses could not have brought it
off. And with *The Feminine Mystique* and *The Second Sex*, too.

But I want to say emphatically that as far as priorities go, our primary concern is to keep those women's presses alive. We cannot depend
on the trade presses to continue publishing our books, after all. I really
feel that some men may get together in a restaurant and say, "Let's
commission an article on the death of the women's movement." Their
basic fear of feminism is stronger than their profit motive. It goes beyond economics. Economics is certainly a major tool of patriarchy, but
when men have to choose between enhancing their economic self-interest and giving power to women, they will choose against their economic self-interest.

J: As they will on a racial issue also.

S: Yes, often. So even though feminist books will continue to be profitable, we cannot complacently trust that the trade presses will act from the profit motive. And it is the existence of the women's presses that will keep our community alive and force the trade presses to publish books by feminists.

J: Yes, I am sure that's one reason why there are beginning to be subsidiaries like Moon Books when it was connected with Random House or the Women's Press relation with Quartet in England, to take advantage of both worlds.

S: But that makes for situations fraught with contradictions, as Moon Books has indeed discovered. I'm not sure that subsidiaries work as a solution. I like better the kind of turnaround that happened with the Shameless Hussy Press, when the distributors came begging for their George Sand translation after the television series renewed people's interest in her work. Shameless Hussy, the only American publisher to have any Sand in print, said to the booksellers, sure you can have as many copies as you want, but only if you are willing to carry our whole line.[2]

J: I *love* that. I hadn't heard about that follow-up. Oh that delights me!

S: And then Shameless Hussy author Ntozake Shange is now a bestseller, so it can be a tribute to the taste and risk taking of the small presses when their authors become more widely known. After all, I get more speaking appointments now, and I always say when I open up the Harper and Row book that it would never have been published if my poems had not been published first by women's presses, and then I list those presses. But from the point of view of my own economic support, being published by a trade house means that I will get more literary grants and be more easily accepted into places like the McDowell Colony.

J: And of course that is important to your development as a writer! Think of Tillie Olsen's *Silences*. There are some other real advantages that need to be mentioned: the trade presses are more likely to bring out parallel hardbound editions for libraries, who often will not buy the same books in paperback. Then there is no getting around it: it is easier for a feminist to get published by Harper and Row if she wants to because our books have built up a certain credibility and context for the next woman writer who comes along. Harper and Row is recognizing the need for, and wants to be recognized as a publisher of, interesting feminist thinkers; its catalog of all these books—I think they're called "women's studies," not "feminist" yet—at any rate shows Harper's pride. And Harper did give a wine reception honoring their women writers at a recent MLA!

S: I think we have to use whatever resources we can command, while remaining aware of the dangers of cooptation and of the necessity for priorities. The first priority is surely to keep our own women's presses healthy. But I think that publishing with a trade house is not by definition destructive and can often help the small presses.

J: Will this do as a conclusion, Susan? or should we say something like: As a conversation this seems pretty one-sided. If a women's press editor or director were with us, for example, there would have been much more dimension and tension.

S: True, and we could enlarge the cast even further to include the readers of this volume. We would very much like to hear from you about any of these issues or about issues we failed to bring up. At least we have introduced you to two good resources: the Feminist Writers' Guild and Shameless Hussy Press.

Notes

1. The Feminist Writers' Guild was formed in 1977 as both a service organization and a political body to represent the needs of feminist writers of all kinds, including technical, creative, and academic. The guild exerts pressure on publishers, newspapers, and foundations regarding prejudice against women as writers on feminism. And the guild works on local and national levels, providing such services as retreats, health insurance, writers' groups, and directories of names and addresses of local feminist writers. For more information write to the guild at P.O. Box 9396, Berkeley, CA 94709.
2. Address of Shameless Hussy, should you want their catalog, is Box 309, Berkeley, CA 94703. Addresses of many other women's presses are included in the Feminist Writers' Guild's first newsletter.

Alternative Publishing

Feminist Presses*

Shirley Frank

Over the past decade, probably one of the most remarkable phenomena in the publishing world has been the proliferation of small, independent presses—among them, perhaps most remarkable of all, feminist presses. The proliferation of small presses is, in part, as Celeste West suggests in *The Passionate Perils of Publishing* (itself the product of a small press, Booklegger Press), a response of the do-your-own-thing generation to the plasticized, commercialized publishing industry created by the many mergers of publishing companies and in particular by their absorption into huge corporations and conglomerates that care less about ideas and literature than about money and profits.[1] Among the legacies of the sixties that the civil rights movement and the antiwar movement bequeathed to the women's movement (most if not all of whose early leaders had been involved in and schooled through the earlier movements) was a growing tradition of politically radical self-publishing, aided by improvements in technology that made it possible for almost anyone to learn how to produce books and journals, so that one or two people working at home could begin and maintain a publishing venture and turn out perfectly respectable-looking books.

No one had more to gain from these developments than women did. Traditionally confined to their homes and, for the past few centuries at least, able to exert influence publicly only through writing—often anonymously—women were clearly ready, with the resurgence of feminism in the 1960s and 1970s, to implement the old adage "The pen is mightier than the sword." They had long had access to pens, not swords, and they were eager to make use of the weapons at hand. "In the late '60s and early '70s," wrote Polly Joan and Andrea Chesman in the introduction to their *Guide to Women's Publishing* (Dustbooks, 1976), the only book-length treatment of the phenomenon of feminist publishing,

> women were more concerned with getting words into print than with distribution. The effort to make the statement, the grit necessary for women writers to overcome the years of patriarchal rejection, to get angry enough to say I AM I AM by publishing a book, starting a women's press, all converged into that magical moment sitting in someone's kitchen or living room surrounded by brown cardboard boxes.[2]

Despite an initial lack of concern about such realities as finances and distribution, Joan and Chesman go on to note,

> the spirit behind a movement can carry it a long way. In the name of sisterhood, friends carted these books across the country to other friends who in turn sold or gave them to other friends. At the same time that feminist presses (books and magazines) were bursting into being, women's print shops were getting off the ground, and women's bookstores began springing up all over the country. The intensity of Feminism as a Movement ... spread through the "printed word." More than any other movement in history, Feminism had been identified with publishing. (pp. 2–3)

It is interesting, though perhaps not surprising, that people who were particularly concerned about education initiated the earliest ventures into feminist publishing. Thus KNOW, Inc., of Pittsburgh, began in 1969 by publishing not only pamphlets and offprints of articles but also the first few volumes of the Female Studies series, volumes that allowed women's studies syllabi to be circulated throughout the country, distributed in the main through the women's caucuses and commissions that were springing up within professional associations in various disciplines. The Feminist Press, founded in 1970, likewise took education for its primary mission, though on a wider scale, publishing books rather than pamphlets. Over the years, the Feminist Press, now with over sixty titles listed in its catalog, has come to be known as a publishing house, but, like KNOW, Inc., it remains a not-for-profit, tax-exempt educational institution, with the publication of books constituting only one part of its educational outreach program. KNOW, Inc., and Feminist Press are the only two feminist presses in the survey that have defined themselves as educational institutions from the beginning. The other presses have defined themselves as profit-making, though few are realizing more profit than is required simply to stay alive and some are now in the process of applying for not-for-profit status in order to become eligible for grants.

One area of feminist publishing that began early and reflected a clearly perceived need to challenge and counter the prevailing sex stereotyping in the education of future generations was children's publishing. Often mothers took the initiative to meet this need. In Princeton, New Jersey, a NOW chapter that called itself Women on Words and Images (WOWI) researched and published *Dick and Jane as Victims,* a pamphlet that as one of the "best-sellers" of the decade was responsible for raising mass consciousness about the sex-biased content of elementary school readers. Another group, in Chapel Hill, North Carolina, formed Lollipop Power, Inc., to produce inexpensive storybooks illustrating nonsexist, nonracist, and alternative family lifestyles. The Feminist Press has also maintained a steady interest in publishing material for children, and it is perhaps no accident that its first publication was a children's book: *The Dragon and the Doctor,* by Barbara Danish.

Despite the early emphasis on education in feminist publishing, more feminist presses today concentrate on creative writing than on educational materials. Many of the small feminist presses were founded by women who were themselves creative writers and whose motivations included publishing their own works as well as those of others—in the tradition, one might say, of the Hogarth Press. There has not been a comparable tendency among writers of critical or scholarly works, perhaps for fairly obvious reasons. Because a good part of the motivation for publishing scholarly works resides in their authors' quest for employment, promotion, or tenure, the value of self-publishing or of publishing with a small feminist press is diminished; the academic establishment is thought, no doubt with justification, to frown on such publication if not to discount it altogether. For the presses the major factor discouraging such publication is economic: the market is minimal, and most feminist presses do not have sufficient "seed money" (unless they receive some grant funding) to produce limited editions of works that will be bought only by a small number of serious scholars and by libraries. In addition, given the extremely constricted budgets within which feminist presses must operate, even those concerned with education must consider carefully whether they want to devote their limited energies and resources to books that will appeal exclusively to an educated elite of scholars and academics or whether they prefer to produce books that will extend feminism to the greatest number of readers possible.

The only feminist press currently publishing scholarly monographs is Eden Press Women's Publications, Inc., Montreal. The Feminist Press and two feminist presses in England—Virago, Ltd., and Women's Press, both in London—publish reprints of feminist classics or "forgotten" literature by women, usually accompanied by a critical or scholarly introduction and sometimes by notes as well. But for the most part, the women's studies scholar seeking to publish her or his dissertation or other research findings must continue to rely on university and other academically oriented presses for publication of book-length manuscripts, although there are several excellent women's studies periodicals in which shorter pieces may find publication.

One development that may improve this situation is a gradual increase in copublishing arrangements that will make the publication of clearly unprofitable, noncommercial books more economical. The Feminist Press, for example, copublished with Indiana University Press *The Female Spectator: English Women Writers before 1800*, edited by Mary Mahl and Helene Koon, an interesting and valuable anthology of early writings that would not attract a large readership. Recently, two feminist presses collaborated across the ocean when Women's Press in England and Feminist Press in the United States copublished *The Convert*, by Elizabeth Robins, a long-overdue reprinting of a novel written by an American woman about the British suffrage movement of the nineteenth century. Such collaboration benefits everyone, inasmuch as it enables two presses together to order a larger print run, which in turn allows a book to be sold at a lower cost.

Even if feminist presses were to publish more scholarly works, possibly with the help of grants, the question would remain for scholars and aspiring academics: would such publication have the "legitimacy" requisite for survival in the "publish-or-perish" world of academe? For creative writers, the benefits of publishing with a feminist press are more evident: access to print for works that might be rejected or heavily edited or censored by commercial publishers; considerably more control over their work than would be allowed by a commercial publisher; possibly better treatment in promoting the book after publication and in keeping it in print without regard to profitability (commercial publishers routinely "remainder" books that do not sell well or readily allow them to go out of print; feminist publishers seldom do, since when they choose to publish a book it is out of a conviction that the book is important rather than out of a belief in the book's earning potential). Books published by feminist presses are not likely to be commercially successful, although there have been occasional modest "best-sellers" (by feminist standards), most notably *Rubyfruit Jungle*, by Rita Mae Brown, published by Daughters, Inc. For a scholarly work, commercial success is, of course, never anticipated; some of the advantages would be as applicable for the scholarly author as for the creative writer if her or his major motive were publication for its own sake without regard to academic credentialing.

An author who does publish with a feminist press will find that, from its perhaps somewhat crude and naive beginnings, feminist publishing has grown increasingly sophisticated, partly because its very growth inspired a certain amount of (flattering) competition from the commercial publishers, who noticed that a market for books by and about women had sprung up ("Over a million copies of feminist press books have been bought," Joan and Chesman noted jubilantly in 1976. "We are supporting nearly 100 feminist bookstores and could support many more" [p. 4]) and who therefore began to "jump on the bandwagon." Today, indeed, there are so many people in the business of publishing "women's books" that it is necessary to distinguish exactly what we do and do not mean by the term "feminist press."

A feminist press can be anything from a relatively long-standing and well-established group of women—usually a collective of some kind—publishing up to forty titles a year, to a lone woman lovingly hand-pressing her solitary book of poems one letter at a time. Between the massive publishing conglomerates pouring forth their "lines" of "women's books," on the one hand, and the self-publishers putting out their own works, on the other, I have tried to put together a list of feminist publishers to whom a potential author might consider submitting a manuscript and to describe something of each press's history, goals, and working methods.

In compiling this list, I found that feminist presses shared certain characteristics that help further to define them as a group. Feminist presses tend to publish works that are "risky," "ahead of society"—usually by several years—and therefore not likely to be "best-sellers." For this reason, in part—and in part because feminist publishers usually have had little money to begin with—a lack of working capital is the major problem that all feminist presses to one degree or another share. Both because of this lack of money—which means that there is typically little left over after production costs are paid to engage in heavy advertising or marketing—and because of the revolutionary content of most of their books, feminist presses usually either do their own distribution, mainly through direct-mail sales, or use feminist or other sympathetic distributors. Often the most decisive way of identifying a feminist press is by observing where its books are sold: although books from commercial publishers may be found in feminist bookstores, few if any books from feminist presses are to be found in ordinary commercial bookstores, particularly the big chain bookstores like Dalton's or Waldenbooks. University bookstores frequently carry books published by feminist presses, especially books ordered by faculty teaching women's studies courses.

Although some feminist presses are technically profit-making businesses while those with a specific educational purpose are not-for-profit organizations, no feminist press I know of is actually making a profit beyond what is needed to pay production costs and, in some cases, modest salaries. Some are not even doing that well, and most are struggling just to stay alive. It is imperative that they do survive, as they offer women—both as writers and as readers—a real alternative to the male-dominated, market-oriented publishing industry that has for so long ignored and neglected serious works by women and will do so again if not reminded by the continued flourishing of feminist presses that there is indeed a market for books by and about women.

The following presses are listed in alphabetical order. Despite their similarities, feminist presses vary considerably in size and scope. Some publish only poetry, while others publish novels. Some publish works aimed at an academic audience; others, a popular audience. Some publish primarily or exclusively works by lesbians; others publish works by men as well as works by women. Not included in this list are small presses run by men, or by men and women, that publish some feminist titles along with their other books, because the listing of any press that ever publishes a feminist book would be well beyond the scope of this article. (To learn more about small presses that do make a point of publishing quality books by women, see Angelika Bammer's "Feminist Texts and the Nonestablishment Press," the next chapter.) Similarly, it would be impossible to list all the "self-publishers" who publish only their own work, even though in every other respect they may qualify as feminist presses.

alicejamesbooks (138 Mt. Auburn St., Cambridge, MA 02138) derives its name from the sister of Henry and William James—a woman entirely eclipsed in her lifetime by her two famous brothers. Unlike other book publishers, alicejamesbooks is a writers' collective that requires authors to join and to become involved in the process of seeing their own books through production. The goal of the press, whose first books appeared in 1974, is to publish, promote, and distribute quality books of poetry, primarily by women. Special concern for the needs of writers is one of alicejamesbooks' long-standing principles, so that a book is not allowed to go out of print as long as there is a demand for it; that is, books are not routinely remaindered. The collective has published over twenty attractive paperbacks (perfect-bound) in four sets or "series," some books combining the works of more than one writer, and has both enjoyed the benefits and grappled with the problems of collectivity as members have come and gone. Although it has published more than one book by the same poet, the collective has a rule that no series will have fewer than half its books by new members. Authors do not receive royalties, because money is ploughed back into the collective to publish new books; they do, however, have the satisfaction of working in a supportive environment and seeing their books appear as they want them to. Writers are involved in all aspects of production, such as design, pricing, and distribution. Indeed, only writers who can fulfill work obligations, including attendance at weekly meetings, can be considered for membership in the collective and hence publication. Therefore, potential authors generally must live in, or be willing to move to, the Boston-Cambridge area. To potential authors who do not live in the vicinity, alicejamesbooks cheerfully suggests that they start their own collective wherever they may live.

The Carolina Wren Press (300 Barclay Rd., Chapel Hill, NC 27504) was founded on 1 January 1976 by Judy Hogan, who remains the editor and publisher. She states that the purpose of the press is

> to provide access to print to writers primarily in North Carolina, but elsewhere, too, doing poetry, drama, fiction. We are publishing the work of writers who are working at the cultural edge, whose writing tends to reshape the way we see the world. As well as having a strong interest in new women's writing, we also are a very supportive press for black Southern writers. There are very few black publishers doing literature.

Thus far, the press has published several books of poetry (including 3 anthologies and 8 individual volumes), beginning with *Chrome Grass,* a collection of poems by Amon Liner (1976), but plans to branch out into other genres and has agreed to publish several novels and one play.

Because the Carolina Wren Press currently has a backlog of accepted manuscripts it is not actively seeking new material at this time, but Hogan says that she is always interested in looking at new work, though sometimes slow in catching up with her correspondence, and that she is "especially interested in thoughtful work that stirs the feelings and reveals old truths about human beingness newly, as well as work sensitive to cultural struggles going on now." She tends to publish authors first in *Hyperion, a Poetry Journal,* so that an editor-author relationship develops before a book is undertaken. Hogan has the last word on whether to accept or reject a manuscript, but she consults with five other board members (all women) on incoming manuscripts. The whole process of evaluating and producing a manuscript can take from two to four years.

Distribution is handled in part through the Writers' Center (Washington, D.C.) and through individual distributors. Print runs are usually one thousand, and reprinting is possible when books sell well. Hogan sells to bookstores locally and through the mail and sends review copies to all the library media journals. She believes that the novels she has accepted "have wide appeal" and wants to get them to a mass market. "I've been pretty fortunate," she writes. "I'm poverty-stricken, but then most small press editors are. I may have more than I realize; I tend to assume it's an uphill battle to bring new good work to people, and tend myself to be optimistic, despite obstacles. But we've had a lot of good response to the books, even if money is still scarce." The principal negative effect of scarce money is that she has a number of books in production waiting to be printed.

When asked what she regards as her most significant achievement, Hogan replies:

> We not only got four new poets (relatively speaking) into print, but have had good attention for them, both in review media, and in some local (WUNC) radio programming. . . . They appeal to a lay audience, especially if presented with conversation about their lives, ideas. I feel really good about the publishing/reading/reaching-the-public phenomena that are beginning to show me my editorial judgment has known what it's been about.

Hogan is also especially proud of a special three-hundred-page women's issue of *Hyperion* that she was able to publish in summer 1980; it contains a mixture of the writings of known and unknown poets, primarily from the South and the Northwest.

Daughters, Inc. (MS 590, P.O. Box 42999, Houston, TX 77042) was founded in 1973 in Plainfield, Vermont, by June Arnold and Parke Bowman. Their purpose was to publish fine fiction by women, and they have succeeded in publishing some twenty novels, many quite innovative and of high literary quality, as well as an anthology of works by young women in high schools (*Daughters in High School*, ed. Frieda Singer) and a collection of essays edited by Charlotte Bunch, *Not by Degrees: Essays in Feminist Education*. Daughters, Inc., was fortunate in "striking it rich" on their first publication, *Rubyfruit Jungle*, by Rita Mae Brown, which did well as a Daughters publication and was subsequently sold to a mass-market paperback publisher for even wider distribution; it is probably the nearest thing to a best-seller that any feminist press has produced. Other writers whose works have been published by Daughters, Inc., include Bertha Harris, Monique Wittig, and June Arnold, whose first novel, *The Cook and the Carpenter*, experiments interestingly with the use of neuter pronouns, leaving the reader to guess through most of the book whether the characters are male or female.

Daughters, Inc., does not consider itself a "lesbian press," according to Joan and Chesman, though people may have the impression that it is, because it has published a number of fine lesbian novels. It does limit its publication program to women, however. After the success of *Ru-*

byfruit Jungle, Daughters, Inc., moved from Vermont to New York City, but it has since moved again—to Texas. It continues to be interested in original, innovative high-quality fiction by women. Now relatively secure financially, the publishers are, according to Joan and Chesman, "in a position to offer solid royalty contracts to women novelists they publish. As such they provide a substantial financial option for women over against . . . commercial trade houses" (p. 126).

Diana Press (4400 Market St., Oakland, CA 94608) was founded in 1972 in Baltimore, Maryland, by a group of women who wanted to develop printing skills. A "lesbian-feminist press," Diana Press limits itself to lesbian writers and has published or reprinted a number of lesbian classics, including selections from *The Ladder, Lesbians' Home Journal, Lesbian Lives* (biographies), and Jeannette Foster's *Sex Variant Women in Literature* (originally published in 1956). It also published Rita Mae Brown's *The Hand That Cradles the Rock* and *Songs to a Handsome Woman,* and numerous other books, all of high quality and attractively produced.

In recent years, however, Diana Press has been plagued with misfortunes. On 25 October 1977, its new Oakland offices (to which it had moved several months earlier) were raided and vandalized. Equipment worth thousands of dollars was ruined (Diana Press had done its own printing and even binding of books), including the mechanicals of upcoming books, so that the press's means of survival was virtually wiped out—along with the morale of its staff. Efforts to raise money from sister presses and other movement organizations were partially successful, at least to the extent of keeping Diana Press alive; but the organization was also plagued with internal tensions and bad publicity, including rumors of lawsuits threatened by disgruntled authors claiming that they or their books had been unfairly treated.

Numerous accusations and counteraccusations that have rippled through the feminist media have made it difficult for anyone not closely involved to be able to figure out the true state of affairs at Diana Press; but in March 1979, Coletta Reid and Kathy Tomyris, who were then running Diana Press (Reid had been doing so since its beginning), distributed a lengthy "overview" letter that summarized the checkered history of the press and announced their decision to forgo their publishing work for a while in favor of getting their business as a printshop viable once more—since they could not "save both."

Because the press is unable to publish even the titles it had accepted for publication, it is evident that Diana Press is not seeking manuscripts. It is, however, seeking funds to publish these remaining works—in particular, the second two volumes of *True to Life Adventure Stories,* edited by Judy Grahn. If the press does get back on its feet, it hopes to resume its activities as a feminist publishing house.

Eden Press Women's Publications, Inc. (245 Victoria Ave., Suite 12, Montreal, Quebec, Canada H3Z 2M6) publishes "original research relating to the new scholarship on women from all academic disciplines." Founded in June 1977 in Montreal, Quebec, Canada, by Sherri Clarkson, the press has already published a number of solid monographs and the first volumes of a periodical, *International Journal of Women's Studies,* and has planned a second journal, *Journal of Women's Studies in Literature.* Eden Press, the parent company, publishes high-quality journals and research reviews in the biomedical sciences. Eden Press Women's Publications, Inc., is a separate, incorporated company that publishes only women's studies materials. Sherri Clarkson remains the general editor.

Eden Press seeks manuscripts that are well written and scholarly, yet interdisciplinary, so that readers from all academic backgrounds can read, understand, enjoy and derive stimulation from the argument, thesis, or reinterpretation. Manuscripts are evaluated by an individual editor and by the general editor. The time lapse between acceptance and publication is generally six months, though it can take much longer if extensive author revision is required. The readership aimed for is "intelligent women and men concerned with the changing role of women and the new scholarship on women." Representative titles include *Birth in Four Cultures, The Dilemma of the Talented Heroine, Virgins, Vamps, and Flappers, Women and American Trade Unions,* and *Daniel Defoe and the Status of Women.* Books are hardcover, with attractive matching red jackets, and sell for between $11 and $15. They are marketed and distributed through direct mail and advertising in relevant journals, through subscription agencies and bookstores. The press is incorporated and "profit-making." According to Sherri Clarkson, however, "there are no profits yet and if there ever are any they will go back into the company."

Eden Press has perhaps somewhat unusual working methods. Initially, as is usual, a one-page summary and a list of chapter headings must be submitted. But once a manuscript is accepted, a revised version incorporating editorial suggestions is submitted, whereupon no changes, deletions, or additions of material are permitted. The press omits the galley stage and therefore must have final versions of manuscripts to work with. It expects authors to cooperate in this policy and also to offer marketing suggestions. It prefers close author-publisher consultations on all aspects of the publishing of a monograph except the technical procedures. Authors receive royalties up to twenty percent on books that sell over two thousand copies. Authors of journal articles cannot be paid. Like all other feminist presses, Eden Press also complains of being "constantly short of money, overworked and understaffed and underpaid." The most significant achievement, Clarkson feels, is the "high quality of the research, writing, and presentation of our monographs and journals."

Effie's Press (1420 45th St., Studio 45, Emeryville, CA 94608) was founded in 1975 by Bonnie Carpenter, a woman who designs and produces limited editions of beautiful letterpress feminist books, including books of poetry by Adrienne Rich and Susan Griffin. Bonnie Carpenter does consider unsolicited manuscripts but usually publishes works by poets she has sought out. She generally prints a limited edition of five hundred copies, of which the author receives ten percent and no royalties. Carpenter supports her efforts by doing free-lance typesetting and design, and she also maintains a painting studio in the same building as her presses. As of 1978 she had produced six titles. Exclusive distribution rights to the books are owned by Serendipity Books (1790 Shattuck Ave., Berkeley, CA 94709).

The Feminist Press (Box 334, Old Westbury, NY 11568) was founded in Baltimore, Maryland, by Florence Howe and Paul Lauter, with a small group of other teachers who early recognized the need for feminist books and materials for the classroom that were not being produced by commercial publishers, who at that time (1970) did not see such publications as being profitable. In fact Feminist Press was started only after efforts to get commercial publishers interested in publishing books by and about women failed, and the group realized that they would have to do it themselves. The Feminist Press began with less than $100 collected from enthusiastic small donors.

The Feminist Press was founded "to rediscover and restore the literary heritage of women to the classroom" and "to change education by creating for children a new kind of literature free of damaging sexual stereotypes." In accordance with the latter aim, the first publication was a children's book, *The Dragon and the Doctor* by Barbara Danish, which appeared in 1971.

Among the rediscovered works of women's fiction that the Feminist Press produced in its early years were Rebecca Harding Davis' *Life in the Iron Mills,* with a biographical-historical introduction by Tillie Olsen; Charlotte Perkins Gilman's *The Yellow Wallpaper,* with an afterword by Elaine Hedges; and Agnes Smedley's *Daughter of Earth,* with an afterword by Paul Lauter. These classics of feminist fiction are kept in print, and they continue to sell well to each new "generation" of students and general readers.

Over the years, the Feminist Press's books have grown increasingly attractive and sophisticated-looking. The press has published an average of four or five books a year, though in one lean year—1977—it was able to publish only one book, *The Maimie Papers.* With the help of grant money, it recently completed production of the twelve-volume Women's Lives/Women's Work series—attractive paperbacks focused on such themes as women and sport, women working in the arts, women working on the land, and women working for social change. Other books in the series include biographies of three "black foremothers" and oral history interviews with a group of Hispanic women in the Southwest. The books, intended as supplementary texts in high school, community college, and college classrooms, are each accompanied by a teaching guide.

The Feminist Press, now planning to publish as many as twelve books a year, continues to seek good materials by and about women, including collections or anthologies of material and, as in the past, potential reprints of the works of lost or neglected women writers. Its Reprints Committee—a group of scholars, teachers, and writers—meets twice annually to review and evaluate the most promising proposals and manuscripts sent in for consideration. Materials by and about minority women are particularly sought. Books recently published or in the planning stages include Paule Marshall's novel *Brown Girl, Brownstones; The Living Is Easy,* a novel by Dorothy West; *Weeds,* a novel by Edith Summers Kelley; *Ripening,* a Meridel Le Sueur reader, edited by Elaine Hedges; *The Silent Partner,* by Elizabeth Stuart Phelps; *Call Home the Heart,* by Fielding Burke; and anthologies of American women's short stories and diaries.

After years of publishing picture books for small children, including the bilingual *My Mother the Mail Carrier/Mí mama la cartera,* Feminist Press is no longer publishing new children's picture books, because they are too expensive to produce at a reasonable price. The press is instead concentrating on the middle-reader range; recent examples include *Tatterhood,* a collection of nonsexist folk and fairy tales; *The Lilith Summer,* a story about a relationship between a young girl and an old woman; and *We Are Mesquakie, We Are One,* a story about an Indian girl.

The Feminist Press also publishes curricular materials, including several volumes of Female Studies (early volumes of this series having been published by KNOW, Inc.); new titles include *Lesbian Women's Studies, Cross-Cultural Women's Studies,* and *All the Women Are White, All the Blacks Are Men, but Some of Us Are Brave: Black Women's Studies.* In addition, the press publishes the *Women's Studies Quarterly* (formerly the *Women's Studies Newsletter*), the newly expanded forty-eight-page official journal of the National Women's Studies Association. The *Quarterly* contains articles and information of interest to women's studies practitioners on every level and in a variety of educational settings.

The Feminist Press is currently preparing a major resource for women selecting an institution of higher education. The result of a long and careful study, the book, called *Everywoman's Guide to Col-*

leges and Universities, will provide information on the quality of life for women (including athletic programs, the curriculum, ancillary services, and so on) at nearly six hundred institutions throughout the United States.

Distribution of Feminist Press books is handled in-house, primarily through direct-mail orders and bulk orders to bookstores, schools, and libraries. Authors are paid royalties. The press lacks sufficient capital to do the amount of marketing and advertising that would significantly increase the sale of books or to do economically large print runs that would bring costs and therefore book prices down. In fact, the press's major problem is insufficient funds to do all the things it wants to do— an ambitious program that includes nonpublishing educational projects such as in-service courses and workshops for teachers and the maintaining of a free reference library and resource center. Its most significant achievement is that it has, without doubt, touched and changed the lives of the thousands of teachers, students, and general readers whom its books, materials, and educational services have reached.

Kitchen Table Women of Color Press (Box 592, Van Brunt Sta., Brooklyn, NY 11215) was founded in September 1981 by Myrna Bain, Hattie Gossett, Audre Lorde, Cherríe Moraga, and Barbara Smith, "to publish the writing of women of color both in the United States and globally." Interested in publishing materials not widely available in the United States, the press intends to publish translations when appropriate. The collective is seeking manuscripts that are concerned about sexism, racism, class oppression, and homophobia and, though not an academic press, will consider research or analysis of relevant issues as well as fiction, poetry, or children's literature falling within its general areas of interest. The group intends to apply for not-for-profit status.

KNOW, Inc. (P.O. Box 86031, Pittsburgh, PA 15221)—whose motto is "Freedom of the Press Belongs to Those Who Own the Press!"—is the oldest feminist press in the country. It was founded in Pittsburgh in 1969 by a group of activist NOW members "to help spread the word about feminism." Specifically its objectives were:

(a) to discuss problems of discrimination wherever they exist, particularly problems of discrimination based on sex; (b) to investigate problems in human rights, particularly those unique to sex-role stereotyping; and (c) to distribute information relevant to the concerns of persons interested in the Women's Liberation Movement.

Since its founding, KNOW, Inc., has published hundreds of pamphlets and a number of books and has reprinted classic feminist articles from the late 1960s and early 1970s. Its first price list, issued in May 1970, listed 19 articles by feminist psychologists, ranging in price from 5¢ to 35¢ apiece. The list has grown to over 350 items, and each year between 10 and 20 new articles and 1 new book are added. The books have been essentially practical works, including studies of sexism in textbooks and several volumes of the Female Studies series (later volumes of this series being published by Feminist Press). Their first book and probable all-time best-seller is *I'm Running Away from Home but I'm Not Allowed to Cross the Street* by Gabrielle Burton.

KNOW, Inc., is looking for ten- to twenty-page pamphlets on a wide range of feminist issues, especially ERA-related materials. Articles are evaluated by individuals, but book-length publications must be approved by committee. The press is run in collective democratic fashion; all employees are paid the same salary. The decision to publish an item can take from one day to two years. Once accepted, pamphlets usually appear within three months; books may take a year or more. Money—or the lack of it—is most often the determining factor.

KNOW, Inc., wants to reach "a general cross-section of people interested in feminism." It distributes books and pamphlets mainly through the mails, places advertisements in selected—most often feminist—publications, and sends its catalog to anyone who asks for one. It is a not-for-profit corporation, and contributions to it are tax-deductible.

"Authors," the press warns, "should not expect to make money from publishing with KNOW, Inc. They can have an unlimited supply of their publication at our retail price. Most book authors invest their own capital to have their book published initially. Payback will be slow." Because the press does not have money to spare, it cannot offer trade discounts on most items, especially pamphlets. It wants to be able to continue to pay staff enough "to keep committed, skilled workers." Locally the press has some difficulty separating itself from NOW, since the members are almost all NOW activists—this confusion means that the phone rings constantly. The members feel that the "establishment of the Female Studies series was very important" and one of their major achievements. "We are also proud that we have stayed viable for ten years, along the way buying equipment and training feminists, which can make us independent. KNOW's equipment, library, extensive files, and experience belong to feminism indefinitely, even if KNOW as KNOW should cease to exist."

Les Femmes Publishing (241 Adrian Rd., Millbrae, CA 94030) was founded in November 1974 by Ruth Kramer. Les Femmes publishes eight to ten nonfiction books a year: history, biography, autobiography, sociology, psychology. Titles have included *The Men behind the Women,* by Jane Miller; *Women of the West,* by Dorothy Gray; *Crimes against Women* (testimony from the International Tribunal of Women held in Brussels in 1976); *Impact ERA: Limitations and Possibilities,* from the California Commission on the Status of Women; and *Differ-*

ent Drummers: They Did What They Wanted, by Antoinette May, biographies of such women as Sarah Bernhardt, Isadora Duncan, Virginia Woodhull, and Amelia Earhart. Les Femmes does consider unsolicited manuscripts and even looks at poetry and fiction. It offers a standard royalty contract for authors. It distributes its books through Celestial Arts, a male-run publishing house of which it is a subsidiary, located at the same address.

Magic Circle Press (10 Hyde Ridge, Weston, CT 06883) was founded in 1972 by Valerie Harms and Adele Aldridge "to achieve financial independence through [women's] arts and to publish work by women." The first publication, which appeared in 1973, was *Notpoems,* by Adele Aldridge. The press has been publishing approximately two books a year, including children's books, a book of poems written by women in prison, and a novel, *A Wreath of Pale White Roses,* by Erika Duncan, which was published with the help of a grant from the National Endowment for the Arts. Magic Circle Press is particularly proud of having published the early work of Anais Nin—sixteen stories written by the author in her early twenties and never before published.

Magic Circle Press is not actively soliciting manuscripts. Individual editors evaluate manuscripts and make decisions within a month. The time span between acceptance and publication of a manuscript is six months. Writers and artists are encouraged to contribute ideas to book design. "Everyone" was the press's reply when asked what readers it was trying to reach. Marketing and distribution are handled through a bigger company: Walker & Co., New York City. The major problem the press has as a feminist press is the familiar one: "not enough acceptance in market," meaning "not enough dough."

Motherroot Publications, Inc. (214 Dewey St., Pittsburgh, PA 15218) was founded in Pittsburgh in 1977 by Anne Pride (formerly of KNOW, Inc.), Paulette Balogh, Felice Newman, Pat McElligott, Mary Alison Rylands, and Janet Lang, who set out "to publish quality work by women." Their first publication, which appeared in July 1977, was *Women and Honor: Some Notes on Lying,* by Adrienne Rich—their all-time best-seller, now in its eighth or ninth printing. Motherroot has published six books so far, at the rate of approximately two a year, including poetry and fiction, and one nonfiction book, *The Uprising of the Twenty Thousand,* about a women's garment strike. The members are not currently seeking new manuscripts; they intend to devote their energies over the next six months to a year to promoting and distributing the books they have already published and to building up their journal, *Motherroot,* a quarterly review of women's work from alternative presses. The journal also contains essays and interviews.

At Motherroot, individual editors evaluate book manuscripts and commit themselves to following through on a project until it is completed. The decision to accept or reject a manuscript is made relatively quickly, and the process of publication is likewise expedited. Editors work closely with authors who have specific ideas about how they want their books to look, and authors always have the right of final approval. Authors sign contracts that ensure royalties, but so far only the Adrienne Rich book has sold enough to earn its author royalties. Motherroot is seeking tax-exempt status, in order to be able to apply for grants as a literary and artistic organization.

Books are distributed through two distributors—Bookslinger and Midwest Distribution—but mainly through direct orders from individual bookstores all over the United States and Canada. Attendance at book fairs and at the display areas of conferences such as the National Women's Studies Association Convention helps promote sales. Many orders come in from *Motherroot,* which is given away at conferences, or on forms sent out with the Adrienne Rich book, which often introduces readers to Motherroot.

Motherroot shares the problem endemic to small presses—lack of sufficient funds. When asked what she regarded as Motherroot's most significant achievement as a feminist press, Paulette Balogh replied:

> Aside from surviving for four years and not going bankrupt, I think that all of the books that we have published—each of them in its own way, because they are for different audiences with different levels of sophistication and feminism—that each of them has made a significant contribution that would not have otherwise been made but for our publishing them.

Naiad Press (7600 Westside Dr., Weatherby Lake, MO 64152) was founded in 1973 by Anyda Marchant, Muriel Crawford, Barbara Grier, and Donna J. McBride, who were all associated with "the late lamented *The Ladder,* famous Lesbian magazine." Barbara Grier (as Gene Damon) "was its editor. . . . When it ceased publication, Anyda and Muriel decided to sink their disability retirement income into a press, specifically a Lesbian Feminist publishing company." The first publication, appearing in 1974, was a lesbian novel, *The Latecomer,* by Sarah Aldridge. Since then the press has published two to four books a year, primarily lesbian fiction, but also some poetry and nonfiction. What it is looking for in particular is "good Lesbian fiction."

Manuscripts are read and evaluated by a "series of readers . . . all women experienced in this work." The process of evaluation usually takes three or four months, "unless it is obvious instantly that the manuscript is unsuitable." Once a manuscript has been accepted, it takes about a year to publish it. The press distributes books itself through mail promotion. Royalty terms are generous—with fifty-percent royalties going to novelists and a slightly smaller percentage to translators. When the actual cost of publishing has been earned back, profits are shared fifty-fifty with the authors, "which may be the highest royalties paid period anywhere," according to Barbara Grier. Indeed, one of their most significant accomplishments, the publishers feel, is "being able to pay our royalties regularly and on time . . . to treat our authors with respect and care. . . ." The other most significant accomplishment, they write, is that they "are very proud of the Vivien books . . . after all, she is one of the most distinguished writers of the twentieth century and she has simply been ignored."

The major problem, as a feminist press, is the familiar one:

We are poor. . . . That is the major problem. We make just enough to keep on publishing . . . it is a hard business . . . costs are outrageous, profit margin almost nonexistent, and the work is demanding. Since we are able to pay no salary we rely on slave labor and the day of the happy slave is fast disappearing. One person now handles all correspondence, 90 percent of the editorial chores, all order filling, recording, and shipping, 90 percent of the bookkeeping. This person also holds down full-time employment, and [she added wryly on our questionnaire form] fills out idiotic forms and vitally important ones like this one . . . and things for Bowker and LC and so on.

Out & Out Books (476 Second St., Brooklyn, NY 11215), founded in 1975 by Joan Larkin, immediately published four books of poetry: *Housework,* by Joan Larkin; *After Touch,* by Jan Clausen; *Periods of Stress,* by Irena Klepfisz; and *Amazon Poetry,* an anthology of lesbian poetry edited by Joan Larkin and Elly Bulkin. The authors themselves produced all these early works, but now the press, operating out of a Brooklyn brownstone, functions for other authors as well, not necessarily authors living in New York. Out & Out Books does not limit itself exclusively to lesbian work, though it does give lesbian work priority. Concerning the press's authors and potential authors, Joan Larkin is quoted in Joan and Chesman's book as saying:

. . . it's hard to predict just what our future will be. I have a strong desire to keep these books, all of which I believe in passionately, in print, and to do some others, more poetry and essays, and maybe a novel. . . . We do not solicit manuscripts! I hardly have time to send things back (for of course people send us tons of unsolicited stuff). I already have a backlog of things I wish I had the time and money to publish. My response to most of the excellent stuff that comes in is the same one Alta gave me when I gave her an early version of *Housework* in 1975: publish it yourself! (p. 158)

Persephone Press (P.O. Box 7222, Watertown, MA 02172) was founded on 24 April 1976 in Watertown, by Pat McGloin, Marianne

Rubenstein, and Gloria Greenfield, whose purpose was "to build an autonomous lesbian-feminist publishing network." Their first publication was *The Feminist Tarot: A View from the Dykes,* by Sally Gearhart and Susan Rennie (1976). As of early 1981 the press had published nine books, covering a variety of subjects and representing a variety of genres. In addition to the tarot book, for example, it published a collection of science fiction stories (*The Wanderground,* by Sally Gearhart); an anthology entitled *Coming Out Stories,* edited by Julia Penelope Stanley and Susan J. Wolfe; *Choices,* a novel about Jewish lesbians, by Nancy Toder; and a nonfiction reprint called *Women, Church and State.* It seeks to publish "innovative and provocative writing" that breaks new ground or fills gaps in the movement—written on subjects that have not yet been explored. Pat McGloin and Gloria Greenfield evaluate manuscripts, usually within thirty days if possible. Once they have the final manuscript in hand, the book may be published within six months.

Although the editors read and evaluate manuscripts from the vantage point of radical lesbian-feminists, they market their books to all readers. For each book they publish, they develop a marketing plan aimed at particular groups of readers. For their latest book, *This Bridge Called My Back,* for example, an anthology of minority women's writings, their marketing strategy stresses appealing to women of color who are not necessarily involved in the movement; feminists, including women of color; women's studies practitioners; and ethnic studies practitioners. Once they have identified potential markets for a book, they pursue appropriate channels, including reviews and advertisements in relevant journals. They also go on book tours.

For the first five years of its life, Persephone did its own distribution, and it still does sixty percent. It has accounts at six hundred bookstores. The press now uses a few distributors, including Bookpeople and the Midwest Distributors, as well as some distributors in Europe and some specialized distributors for certain books.

Persephone Press is profit-making and professionally oriented. Authors receive contracts and royalties. Because it is specifically a lesbian press, it does not have access to traditional sources of capital, such as banks; however, as the press grows more successful, the editors expect this problem to diminish. Persephone Press has been favorably noted in the media as an up-and-coming press that may well emerge as a leader among small presses in the nation (see, e.g., the *West Coast Review of Books,* Jan.–Feb. 1981). This image exists, in large part, because Gloria Greenfield and Pat McGloin have committed themselves to making the press successful and feel strongly that they know how to select manuscripts according to what they think is important and then how to market their books with integrity. They are proud that although approximately 90% of all books published do not sell as many as 5,000 copies, 75% of Persephone's books have sold more than 5,000 copies in their first year. The novel *Choices* sold 5,000 copies in only twelve weeks. *The Wanderground* has sold over 16,000 copies and has been translated into Danish and German—with Swedish and Norwegian translation rights now in the offing.

In addition to regular marketing of their books, Persephone Press has initiated a book club, which allows those who want to support the press by joining to purchase books at a twenty-five percent discount, and *Persephone Review*, a lesbian writers' quarterly with information about grants, publishing houses, and other matters of interest.

The Seal Press (533 11th East, Seattle, WA 98102) was founded in 1976 by Rachel da Silva and Barbara Wilson to print "regional feminist work"—particularly the work of feminists in the Northwest. Their first publication, in August 1976, was *Private Gallery*, a book of poetry by Melinda Mueller. The press has since published eighteen books, including a number of small poetry chapbooks. It has published, and is looking for, a variety of genres and topics. Publications include books of poetry and fiction, an autobiography, children's books, a collection of essays, and, most recently, a self-help book for battered women.

A collective of three people evaluates manuscripts, usually within a couple of weeks, and the time span between acceptance and publication varies between six months and a year, depending on the book. The readership the press is trying to reach is "ideally, everyone," that is, "English-speaking people in the United States and Canada," and not just women. It uses several distributors, including Bookpeople, Wordswork in the Northwest region, Crossing Press on the East Coast, and Madrona Press for one book. It also uses mail-order advertising. The press is not-for-profit and is trying to get tax-exempt status.

Contracts with authors have varied for different books. Some authors have received royalties, others a percentage of the books, and still others a flat fee on grant money. Authors do not usually involve themselves in book production but do call up once in a while to find out how things are going.

Barbara Wilson, one of the cofounders, feels that Seal Press does not have special problems because it is a feminist press but that, on the contrary, the liberal city of Seattle offers a supportive environment. "Everyone thinks it's nice," she says, "that these three 'girls' can have a press of their own." When asked what she regarded as Seal Press's most significant accomplishment, she joked, "Aside from not murdering each other . . . ," but then added that it was the republication of the Anna Louise Strong autobiography (originally published in 1935), *I Change Worlds*, an important work of over 460 pages that was expensive to produce without the help of grants.

Shameless Hussy Press (P.O. Box 424, San Lorenzo, CA 94580) was founded and is still run by Alta, who began by publishing her own works and those of Lyn Lyfshin and Susan Griffin in inexpensive, stapled form. She has moved on to more attractive, perfect-bound books but continues to publish unusual or innovative material. Shameless Hussy was the first press to publish Ntozake Shange's *For Colored Girls*—before anyone else recognized its value. Other publications have included a volume of Calamity Jane's letters to her daughter and a reprint of an out-of-print English translation of George Sand, featuring original etchings.

Spinsters, Ink (R.D. 1, Argyle, NY 12809), founded and operated by Maureen Brady and Judith McDaniel, published its first two books in February 1979: *Give Me Your Good Ear,* a novel by Maureen Brady, and *Reconstituting the World: The Poetry and Vision of Adrienne Rich*, a monograph by Judith McDaniel. The next two books planned for publication are *The Cancer Journals,* a collection of essays by Audre Lorde, and *Bones & Kim,* a novel by Lynn Strongin. In a letter sent to friends and potential friends in August 1980, however, the two publishers indicated that they needed help to support the production of these two books. "Although we sold out the first printings" of the first two books, they wrote, "we found that we had to borrow money to pay for the second printings. Due to escalating costs of printing and paper we cannot even anticipate earning a profit on these books without raising their cover prices, something we are reluctant to do. This is despite the fact that the work of Spinsters, Ink is all volunteer effort." They have "become more grounded," they state, "in the realities of feminist press publishing: we are applying for not-for-profit status and are hoping that we may support some of our efforts in the future with grant funding."

Sunbury Press (Box 274, Jerome Sta., Bronx, NY 10468) publishes a triquarterly journal, *Sunbury,* and several books of poetry. The publisher, Virginia Scott, is interested in publishing excellent work by poets who would not receive adequate treatment elsewhere; therefore, she actively solicits work by women poets, minority poets, and working-class poets. The magazine contains poetry by men as well as by women, but so far the books have all been by women, including chapbooks by Virginia Scott, Kathleen Meagher, Lorraine Sutton (*SAYcred LAYdy*), Jodi Braxton (*Sometimes I Think of Maryland*), and Fay Chiang (*Poems*). Back issues of the magazine, which are more like anthologies of poetry, are marketed like books. Distribution has been handled in part through COSMEP/South. Sunbury, which has depended on government grants, is, according to Joan and Chesman, in "the process of becoming a non-profit, tax-exempt corporation which will enable them to solicit money from private foundations and persons.

They also are at the start of a two-year sales subscription and promotion effort" (p. 165). The press actively sponsors readings and promotional events in cities where they have editors: New York, San
Francisco, Cleveland, and Buffalo. About the need for fiscal responsibility, they are quoted (by Joan and Chesman) as saying:

> We've learned that it ain't just editing and publishing. It's business
> sense, annual fiscal statements, responsible and continuing compe-
> tent administration. Sunbury Press is growing as a feminist press in
> its fourth year. (p. 166)

The Vanity Press (Box 15064, Atlanta, GA 30383)—whose logo is a
peacock—was founded in Atlanta, Georgia, in 1975, by Sonya Jones
and Lydia Anne Moore, "to provide a feminist alternative to 'New
York the goat' [sic]." It published its first books the same year: *The Ultimate Dare* (poems), by Sonya Jones, and *Yesterday's Kill* (poems), by
Lydia Anne Moore. Since then, approximately two books per year
have appeared, including novels, short stories, and a dramatic monologue. Manuscripts are evaluated by an editorial board ranging from
working-class women to university professors. The Vanity Press is looking in particular for fiction by southern women. They are trying to
reach women readers primarily "but all who are interested in quality
literature." It can take between one and six months to accept a manuscript, during which time, however, constant contact is maintained
with the author. If a manuscript is rejected, Sonya Jones returns it with
detailed comments. If it is accepted, it usually appears within a year.
Authors, writes Jones, "should be prepared for gentle, but extensive,
criticism." They should also be "prepared for time-lags, as few people
can do only so much." The press has "no dealings with agents."

Sonya Jones lists as the Vanity Press's three major problems: (1)
money, (2) establishment-bookstore acceptance, and (3) time—"personnel involved all work at other jobs. . . ." She considers the press's
most significant achievement the very fact "that we were founded and
still are in the heart of the South."

Violet Press (Box 398, New York, NY 10009) is a lesbian-feminist
press that has been publishing poetry since 1971. Among its titles are
Dyke Jacket and *Poems and Songs,* by Fran Winant; *To Lesbians Everywhere,* by Judy Greenspan; *We Are All Lesbians,* a poetry anthology; and *Medusa Music,* by Flash Silvermoon. Fran Winant is currently
doing the work alone and, according to her comments in Joan and
Chesman's *Guide,* is finding survival difficult: "It is *not* surviving financially," she reports, "even though the books are well distributed . . .
all are getting sold . . . and the prices are higher than I'd like them to
be. . . . There would be royalties if there were profits but there aren't."
Winant is interested, according to the same report, in doing some trav-

eling and reading and in doing "a book about how to get your feminist act on the road"—with input from many women who've been there (p. 173).

Virago, Ltd. (Ely House, 37 Dover St., London Wl, England) was founded in 1973 by Carmen Callil, who operated the new business from her flat in London. The first publication was *Fenwomen: A Portrait of Women in an English Village,* by Mary Chamberlain, published in September 1975. At first associated with Quartet Books, Ltd., another publishing house, Virago Limited became independent in January 1977, with the help of a bank loan. Since then, the four women who constitute the staff have managed to publish a phenomenal number of books: ten titles in 1977, twenty-three in 1978. They plan to "work up to" thirty titles per year. The books have covered social history, autobiography and biography, fiction, sociology, social questions, education, history, health and reference, and literary criticism. Many of the works are reprints, particularly of books recently published in the United States, such as *Sexual Politics, Of Woman Born,* or *Daughter of Earth.* Others are historical reprints, like *The Suffragette Movement* by Sylvia Pankhurst or *Love of Worker Bees* by Alexandra Kollontai. Virago particularly seeks original fiction and serious feminist analysis as well as good biographies. The press uses readers, but the final decision to publish is made either by Carmen Callil, the managing director, or by Ursula Owen, the editorial director, or by both. With reprints they usually make their decision quickly, perhaps within a month; unsolicited manuscripts take longer. They also commission many of their books. Once a book has been accepted, it takes from nine months to a year to publish it—less time, again, for reprints.

Virago, Ltd., was founded with the idea of publishing not only for the women's movement but for a general audience, so that feminist ideas "could be disseminated as widely as possible." Though the general audience the founders desired to some extent exists, the books may appeal more to an academic audience and particularly to women, especially feminists. Distribution is handled in the United Kingdom through Wildwood House—another publishing house, with its own sales force. Virago sells overseas through various outlets, with which it deals directly from its office. The press considers itself a profit-making organization, but because it is still paying off an initial loan, salaries are modest and authorial advances low. Lack of funds means the press is understaffed and not always able to answer authors as quickly as it would like to. In addition to four staff members, the press has an advisory group of about thirty women, who meet twice a year and suggest books, read manuscripts, and offer general advice.

Problems that Virago, Ltd., feels it has experienced because it is a feminist press have included suspicion both from the "outside world" and from within the women's movement. It has "the usual financial problems," as a staff member put it. "On the whole, though," she adds, "being a feminist press has been a source of strength: it gives a unity to the list and whilst there is a lot of opposition, one also gets an enormous amount of help." The press feels that its most significant achievement has been "infiltration": "Our books are reviewed and sold in the normal way; people seem to like what we're doing. As we believe that everything we publish represents some aspect or view which is feminist, we hope then that we're helping to influence and change social attitudes and opinions."

Womanpress (Box 59330, Chicago, IL 60645) was founded in 1974 in Chicago by Marie Kuda "to publish an annotated bibliography of lesbian literature; to disseminate information on lesbian culture and history." Its first publication, *Women Loving Women: An Annotated Bibliography of Women Loving Women in Literature,* appeared in September 1974, and it has published one or two books annually since, including poetry and monographs. Womanpress is not currently soliciting manuscripts; it has an anthology and two novels under contract. Manuscripts are "read by the editor and one or more literate friends," who take approximately a month to decide whether to accept or reject a manuscript and one to two years to publish it if accepted. The readers that Womanpress wants to reach are "women, particularly lesbians, who desire to know more of the lesbian literary heritage/contribution to arts in English." Books are distributed through direct sales to libraries, universities, and bookstores; through direct-mail advertising, reviews, and so on; and through distributors.

Womanpress lists as its major problems:
Undercapitalization, shared with most small businesses. Lack of a solid, thriving distributor of women's materials. As a lesbian press, heavy first-class mail expenses on direct mail pieces to individuals and shipping bags, etc., to prevent "see through" for those customers who require confidentiality. Lack of accessible mailing lists for direct mail advertising due to confidentiality requirements of most organizations that have large lesbian membership.

Womanpress's most significant achievements, its founder feels, have been: "Publication of the *first* annotated bibliography of lesbian literature. Followed closely by Womanpress's sponsorship of five annual lesbian writers' conferences (1974–78) attended by over 1,000 lesbian-feminist writers/authors/poets from all over the country, Canada, and England."

The Women's Press, Ltd. (124 Shoreditch High St., London, England El 6JE) was founded in 1977 in London, by Stephanie Dowrick, Sybil Grundberg, and Quartet Books, Ltd. (with which Women's Press is an associated, autonomous company). The founders sought "to foster new writing with a conscious feminist perspective and to publish that writing with the same perspective" and "to make available to a contemporary audience historical feminist writing." The first publications, which appeared in February 1978, were *Aurora Leigh & Other Poems* by Elizabeth Barrett Browning, edited by Cora Kaplan; *Love and Freindship* by Jane Austen; *Lolly Willowes* by Sylvia Townsend; *Lives of Girls & Women* by Alice Munro; and *The Awakening* by Kate Chopin, edited by Helen Taylor. The Women's Press, Ltd., is "especially interested in fiction, literary history, art history, physical and mental health, politics" and intends to publish sixteen to twenty new titles each year. Stephanie Dowrick, Sibyl Grundberg, and (since September 1978) Niki Honore evaluate manuscripts, and they try to reach a decision within six months. Once a manuscript has been accepted, publication may follow in as little as seven months. Concerning their way of working with authors, the editors write:

> We want to involve our authors as much as possible in the actual process of the production of thcir work, breaking down the usual power relationships of the publishing world. We try to combine a constantly evaluated political perspective with extremely high "professional" standards. We do feel a commitment to our authors as writers with long careers; i.e., we are not interested in a single book as a single "product."

The Women's Press aims to reach "always a double audience: feminists *and* the general reader in whichever area we are publishing. We do want feminist ideas widely disseminated through our books." They explain that they are "owned 51% by Quartet Books, Ltd.—a fairly small publishing house . . . with a strong commitment in the areas of politics, social history, and literature—and work autonomously up to the stage of marketing," at which point they use Quartet's sales force and agents. The Women's Press, which hopes to be profit-making, also sells books directly from its own office.

When asked what problems Women's Press has because it is a feminist press, the editors answered that it was "difficult to know" at an early stage of development "which are difficulties particular to a feminist press or which are general difficulties for a very small, new press. We do very much regret," they added, "that there are no feminist bookstores in Britain and that the feminist journals have very tiny circulations." In 1980, however, The Women's Press, Ltd., realized what may become one of the advantages of being a feminist press when it copublished, with Feminist Press in New York, Elizabeth Robins' suffragist novel *The Convert*, edited with an introduction by Jane Marcus.

Two years ago, when asked what they regarded as the most significant achievements of Women's Press, aside from "our very existence in the face of some real difficulties," the editors singled out their calendar, "*Working Women Artists,* which shows the work of twelve contemporary painters, sculptors, a photographer and collage artist from Britain, the United States, and Europe. It is the first time," they noted, "that contemporary artists' work has been put together in an expensive, full-colour, *immodest* way, putting women's art on walls everywhere, we hope!"

In addition to feminist presses dedicated to publishing works intended for adult readers, there are those devoted to publishing feminist literature for children. Among them, in addition to Feminist Press (q.v.), are:

Lollipop Power, Inc. (P.O. Box 1171, Chapel Hill, NC 27514) was founded in 1969 (incorporated in 1970) by a feminist collective concerned with counteracting the sex stereotyping prevalent in children's books. In addition to presenting girls and boys in ways that are not sex-stereotyped, Lollipop Power's books also show a variety of family styles, including single-parent families, mothers who work outside the home, children who are cared for in day-care centers, nurturant fathers, and people of various races and cultures.

Since 1970, Lollipop Power has published over a dozen books for preschool and elementary school children. The members of the collective state that their "priority now is on publishing manuscripts which have a definite feminist theme, as opposed to books which are just 'nonsexist.' " Other priorities include strong female protagonists, especially black, Hispanic, or Native American girls and women; females struggling to change values and behaviors; friendship and solidarity among girls and women; nonheterosexist values; nontraditional family situations. Although they have published only fiction, they would be interested in receiving nonfiction, especially biographies for children.

Lollipop Power is incorporated as a not-for-profit, tax-exempt literary and educational organization. The nonhierarchical collective, with approximately ten members at a given time, shares decisions and rotates responsibilities as much as possible. When Lollipop Power started, neither collective members nor authors and illustrators were paid for their work; now, small payments are made to authors and illustrators and to people performing specific jobs, although editorial work is still done on a volunteer basis.

When a manuscript is received, it is read by one woman, who weeds out inappropriate manuscripts; those that are appropriate are then passed on to at least two additional readers. If accepted, a manuscript then proceeds to the workshop stage:

> We work collectively, which sometimes makes our decision-making processes comparatively slow. We also workshop [sic] manuscripts

extensively, which often results in requests for substantial revision. The other side of that coin is that when we think a manuscript has potential we're willing to invest a great deal of our own time in working with the author to make it publishable.

Once a manuscript has been accepted by the board, an illustrator is sought, unless the author has provided her or his own illustrations, from people who have written expressing an interest in illustrating Lollipop Power's books. When completed, the final product goes to the board for review and, if approved, it goes to press as soon as possible. The whole process can take as little as six months, if the author is also the illustrator, but it usually takes about eighteen months.

Lollipop Power's ideal audience is all children. The collective does most of its own distribution but also sells through several distributors. It has found that direct mailing is the most successful form of advertising. It experiences the usual difficulties of a small press, including difficulty in getting reviews or exposure, and the high costs of small print runs. When asked what they regard as their most significant achievements as a feminist press, the members of the collective replied:

> Probably that we've endured. That feminist presses and feminist press publications are not ephemera but that we've continued to publish and to adapt the collective process for nearly ten years. That we have met and are continuing to meet a need that would never be met through previously existing male-dominated institutions.

New Seed Press (P.O. Box 3016, Stanford, CA 94305) was founded in Madison, Wisconsin, in 1972, by a group of parents and teachers at a new, parent-controlled free school in order to raise funds and to provide nonsexist materials for the school. The first publication, in 1972, was called *Margo Makes a Mess.* Since then the press has published over half a dozen antisexist, antiracist books. The kinds of manuscripts it seeks have

> feminist content: stories with active female characters who take responsibility for themselves and their lives; stories that challenge assumptions about the inferiority of women and Third World peoples; stories that depict realistic situations and conflicts in children's lives; stories of women working for social change; stories that convey the message that people can struggle together to change their world.

It is also seeking "manuscripts for and about children living in supportive living situations with lesbian adults."

New Seed Press is "a not-for-profit feminist collective." Everyone in the collective reads and evaluates manuscripts, and decisions are made by consensus. The decision-making process usually takes one month, and the time between acceptance and publication varies between four and ten months, "depending on finances, staff energy, how much the manuscript needs to be changed, how complicated the illustrations/ designs are, etc."

The readers New Seed Press is trying to reach are "children, librarians, teachers, parents." Although it is primarily a mail-order press, it also uses small movement distributors. The members are currently putting more energy into the school and library market. They regard as their most significant achievements "Survival; development of skills; the publication of *Frances Ann Speaks Out: My Father Raped Me;* working collectively. . . ."

Notes

*I wish to thank Florence Howe and Frances Kelley for their help in preparing the original questionnaire that went out to all known feminist publishing houses and Florence Howe for her valuable critique of the manuscript at a later stage of its development. I also wish to thank Joan E. Hartman and Ellen Messer-Davidow, the editors of this volume, for their useful comments and, above all, for their patience.

1. Celeste West and Valerie Wheat, *The Passionate Perils of Publishing* (San Francisco: Booklegger, 1978).
2. Polly Joan and Andrea Chesman, *Guide to Women's Publishing* (Paradise, Calif.: Dustbooks, 1976), p. 2; further references to this book are cited in the text. All other quotations in this article are taken from answers to the questionnaire or to telephone interviews.

Feminist Texts and the Nonestablishment Press

Angelika Bammer

For feminists who write, whether as artists, scholars, or activists, publication presents a dilemma. Our words cannot remain silent, hidden in drawers, if we want to take our place as active members of the literary and academic communities. Yet the commercial and academic publishing industries want texts that will serve their particular political and economic interests. How then can we, as feminist writers, pay the dues exacted for official validation as published authors without selling out our principles? How can we resolve the conflict between our political need to resist cooptation of ourselves and our work by established institutions and our economic need to survive on the terrain dominated by these institutions? If we want to publish with integrity, we must find publishers who share our interests and goals. But who besides the feminist presses is there?

It seemed to me that our most likely allies would be the small presses and the alternative presses. For these "nonestablishment" presses (as I shall call them) who, whether by choice or by necessity, exist on the margins of the empire dominated by the large and established publishers, have a necessarily ambivalent relationship to the publishing industry, of which they are themselves a part. Like feminist scholars in academia, they represent a locus of contradiction within and potential resistance to the larger structure in which they are embedded. Thus, I began with two basic questions: Are nonestablishment

117

presses interested in feminist texts? Are feminists interested in small and alternative presses?

I decided to begin with a survey of small and alternative presses. Yet this was more easily said than done. For not only do most directories list only the larger publishers, but the ephemeral existence of nonestablishment presses makes accurate record keeping virtually impossible.

The ground-breaking work of Len Fulton and Ellen Ferber, editors of the *International Directory of Little Magazines and Small Presses* (14th ed. [Paradise, Calif.: Dustbooks, 1978–79]), has produced the only comprehensive listing of small presses to date. *Alternatives in Print* (5th ed. [San Francisco, Calif.: Glide Publications, 1977–78]), compiled by a task force on social responsibilities of the American Library Association, is a more specialized listing of small political and countercultural presses, including the materials the presses publish and the bookstores that serve as their distributors. These two directories were my primary sources. In addition, I selected a few specialist presses from the *International Academic and Specialist Publisher's Directory* (Tim Clarke, ed. [New York: Bowker, 1975]). Although the specialist presses are technically neither small nor alternative, they depart in goal and in scope from mainstream academic and commercial publishing and are thus often omitted from regular directories.

The principles I used in selecting the presses to be surveyed reflect my assessment of the wide-ranging publishing interests of feminist scholars in modern languages. I chose every press that published research or criticism in the field of language and literature as well as presses that published in related areas such as contemporary culture, film, mass media, pedagogy, and critical theory. Because research by and about women in minority cultures and the third world has suffered particular neglect and resistance in academic publishing, I made a special effort to identify publishers who appeared responsive to these concerns. Finally, I picked a representative sampling of creative writing presses, not only because creative writing is the mainstay of small press publishing but also because many feminist scholars are also writers with an interest in gaining recognition for their creative work. Each of the presses selected had to be "viable," that is, its publishing record over the last few years had to indicate that it was stable or expanding; it had to have published at least two booklength texts in an average year, and it had to be other than a vanity press. Despite the concentration of nonestablishment presses in California, I decided to choose presses throughout the United States and Canada. I did not attempt to provide a complete or accurate reflection of the general publishing patterns characteristic of small and alternative presses. My purpose was specific: I wanted to determine the presses' general receptivity to feminist texts and to identify those in particular whose politics and policies suggested that they might offer viable publishing opportunities for feminists.

My survey included one hundred small, alternative, and specialist presses. Each received a three-page questionnaire with twenty-seven questions addressing the press's publishing interests, projected readership, the composition and decision-making process of its editorial board, procedures for manuscript submission and evaluation, payment policies, ideological orientation, and sources of income (Appendix A). Most of the questions were factual with multiple answers. I did ask some opinion questions, however, in order to test the publishers' reactions to the political nature of a manuscript, particularly a feminist one. In order to screen out statements that reflected current political etiquette rather than the actual publishing interests of a press, I probed the issue of a press's ideological orientation through a cluster of separate questions. By cross-checking answers, I hoped to assess a press's position more realistically.

A total of forty-six publishers responded to the survey. Many added comments on the questionnaire and enclosed lists of their publications. I interpret this high rate of response and the willingness, even eagerness, to provide information as an indication of an active interest on the part of these presses in communicating with feminist scholars and writers. From the total number of respondents I have selected for more detailed discussion those presses that offered what I thought were genuine publishing possibilities for feminist literature and/or scholarship.[1]

The concept of a nonestablishment press allowed me to group together a number of otherwise quite different publishing traditions. First there is the small press, conceived in protest against an age of indiscriminate mass reproduction. The small press bears the traits of its ancestor, the exclusive private press, in its love for fine printing and its loyalty to the experimental avant-garde of creative writers. Although its impulse to salvage the beautiful can regress into nostalgia, it also embodies an element of resistance. This dissident voice links the small press to the more consciously political alternative press, whose primary goal is socioeconomic change. While the small press allows an aesthetic opposition to be heard, the alternative press voices political dissent. Finally, there are those nonestablishment presses oriented toward scholarly publishing who tend to see themselves and their authors as scholars rather than as artists or activists. Some of the presses in this category actually compete with academic and specialist publishers, and thus regard their own nonestablishment status as merely transitory.

A common ideological and material base unites all these presses and extends beyond their differences. By publishing material that established presses reject as "too political" or "too experimental," nonestablishment presses serve an important cultural-political function by giving those who have been denied a public voice a chance to speak. In this sense, they are *all* alternative. Publishing those not published elsewhere, nonestablishment presses tend to be small, for there is usually a direct correlation between the size of a press and the fame of those it publishes. The presses I surveyed, for example, typically have between two and three people on their editorial boards and publish an average of five to six texts (excluding periodicals) a year. Since this total includes such publications as chapbooks and political pamphlets, the number of actual book-length texts is smaller still.

The political choice of allowing the unknown to say the unpopular has an important economic consequence: it brings in little if any money. Yet even nonestablishment presses must make a living. Precisely because they are independent (unlike academic presses, only four of the forty-six presses that responded to the survey are supported by institutions), nonestablishment presses must be commercial. Thus, almost half (48%) emphasize that sales are their major or sole source of income. The hand-to-mouth existence of many small presses determines their ability to pay their authors. Responses indicate that advances are rare and modest; royalties are either low (averaging 10%), shared (13% of the respondents pay on the tentative basis of "when book earns money, we share it"), or not paid at all (21% of respondents pay only in copies). Many small presses require subsidies by their editors, publishers, and sometimes, authors,[2] for the price of being alternative is economic marginality. The subsistence-level economy of a small press ultimately determines what it can publish; it cannot afford to publish works for which there is no market. Therefore, it is significant that sixty-one percent of the respondents to the survey assess the marketability of feminist research favorably.[3] Over half of the respondents (57%) say that they will consider publishing such research; many who respond negatively feel compelled to explain or qualify their rejection. This close correlation between marketing interests and publishing interests lends a reassuring note of pragmatism to the positive response of nonestablishment presses to feminist writings. Economic considerations generally temper, if not determine, the politics of publishing, and if feminist works are now being welcomed it may be because to reject them no longer makes good economic sense.

Economic marginality has an advantage: "free" of accountability to external funding institutions or internal staffs, editors can make independent choices. Over half the respondents indicate that editorial decisions are made by the editor or publisher alone and that additional readers are rarely consulted. This autonomy allows a supportive editor to publish women's writings regardless of the general orientation of the press. For instance, though Press Pacifica (P.O. Box 47, Kailua, HI 96734) concentrates on Hawaiana, its editor, who is interested in women's studies material (especially women's history and reprints), published a work by Elizabeth Cady Stanton and donated the proceeds to the ERA. Since the personal interests of editors will thus affect their publishing decisions, the constitution of editorial boards—the absence or presence of women in these positions—becomes crucial. While few of the responding presses have no women on their editorial boards, few have more than one. Male editors, then, usually constitute the decision-making majority, particularly in those presses publishing scholarly writings, where men outnumber women on editorial boards three to one.

On the basis of their different orientations I divide the respondents to the survey into three groups—art presses, activist presses, scholarly presses. The determining factors are what a press publishes, whom it wants to reach, and what effect it wants to have on society. Of course presses, like writers and texts, can never be reduced to a single dimension or type; we can be creative, politically committed, and scholarly all at the same time. Our individual emphases, however, will differ and shift. Therefore, my categories suggest emphases; they should not be seen as rigid or opposing.

Art Presses

The returns indicate that almost half of the respondents publish creative writings. While some, in their publishing emphases and goals, belong with either the scholarly or the activist presses, seventeen presses (37% of total respondents) form a relatively cohesive group of art presses. Frequently run by artists, these presses publish creative work (mostly poetry) of contemporary, often local, writers. The one social goal they all agree on is the desire to improve aesthetic appreciation. Yet over half express an additional sense of social responsibility in their wish to disseminate information and further critical thinking. They see themselves as apolitical, but open-minded. Thus, although they are virtually unanimous in rejecting a prescriptive stance, not one of them objects to a text simply because it has an overt political tendency.

Because my survey questions were oriented more toward scholarly than toward creative writing, art presses had to adapt their responses to the given format. Despite this limitation, however, I interpret their stated response to feminist research as an indication of their receptivity to feminist texts in general. The attitudes they express are ambivalent, if not contradictory. Although art presses unanimously assess feminist work as viable and important, a surprisingly large proportion

(41%) regard it as a fad. Needless to say this attitude calls into question the seriousness with which they might evaluate a feminist manuscript. Nevertheless, almost half the presses in this group reply that they will consider publishing feminist texts.

Such contradictions seem to reflect many art presses' basic unawareness of their own ideological positions. One press, for instance, questions the validity of women's studies as a discipline; another agrees to consider the work of cultural minorities, such as women or ethnic groups, only if their minority perspective "does not obtrude." Yet neither sees a contradiction in simultaneously claiming complete objectivity. In fact, even though almost every press in this group denies, more or less emphatically, that any biases deflect its perception of a manuscript's intrinsic merits, few have actually published feminist materials. This fact applies even to those presses whose avowed purpose is the publication of writers in groups whose works have traditionally been ignored. A Canadian publisher of creative writings by children and youth, All about Us/Nous Autres, Inc., has published a single book with a focus on girls and young women as an International Women's Year project. The editor of Casa Editorial, publisher of Hispanic writers and texts on Latin culture, says that she supports our work but that feminism is outside her purview. Place of Herons, which publishes Native American and "6th world poets," insists that enough feminist material is published already.

Among those art presses that indicate an interest in publishing feminist works, several do so with considerable ambivalence. These are Croissant & Co. (c/o D. Schneier, Ohio Univ., Dept. of English, Ellis Hall, Athens 45701), Northwoods Press, Inc. (R.D. #1, Meadows of Dan, VA 24120), Swamp Press (4 Bugbee Rd, Oneonta, NY 13820), and the Washoe Press/the Sempervirens Press (P.O. Box 91922, Los Angeles, CA 90009). Croissant & Co. (which has also published monographs on Thomas Wolfe) and Swamp Press (which "wouldn't reject even an academic manuscript if it was good") will also consider works of a critical nature, while the Washoe Press is interested in philosophical and experimental writings ("the odd ones that are as rare as yetis"). Yet since all four of these presses concur that feminist writing is basically a fad and not even an easily marketable one, it would seem that their professed receptivity to feminist manuscripts reflects a theoretical stance rather than an actual publishing commitment.

Three presses in the art group do encourage and solicit feminist writings: the Bieler Press (4603 Shore Acres Rd., Madison, WI 53716), Contraband (P.O. Box 4073, Sta. "A," Portland, ME 04101), and Harold House, Publishers (2144 Harold House St., Houston, TX 77098). Their publication output is slim; Bieler and Contraband publish a mere two texts in an average year and Harold House between four and six.

While all three are primarily publishers of creative writers, their interests vary: Contraband also considers criticism in the field of contemporary literature, Harold House publishes monographs, and Bieler specializes in finely printed editions. All are interested in innovative writings and in underpublished writers. Of perhaps greatest import for feminists is their political stance. While Harold House claims to be "apolitical," their strong support of feminist writings is actually far from neutral; Bieler and Contraband both acknowledge that neither the writer nor the reading of texts can be "devoid of ideology" (Bieler). This awareness of their own bias, in conjunction with their strong validation of feminist work, lends credibility to their expressed interest in publishing such texts. The invitations of all three of these presses for feminist manuscripts thus seem sincere.

Activist Presses

I classify as activist those eleven presses (24% of total respondents) whose primary emphasis is social change and whose acknowledgment of the politics of publishing distinguishes them from the presses in the other two groups. While artist and scholarly presses often simply ignored the questions concerning their ideological perspectives, each of the activist presses responded, defining their position in sociopolitical terms. They repudiate the claim that a work may be judged solely on the basis of its intrinsic merits, and they insist that a writer's ideological assumptions be explicit in the text. The activist presses work within the context of the left—for the rights of working people, minority groups, third world peoples and for cultural, political, and economic freedom of all people. The one social goal they all share is the promotion of socioeconomic change.

Their publishing interests reflect their belief in knowledge and critical analysis as primary tools for achieving this goal. Thus, all but one of the activist presses publish scholarly research and those who publish creative writings do so in conjunction with critical or theoretical texts. The function of art and research must be assessed by a radical critique of the total cultural apparatus—this understanding underlies the emphasis of activist presses on critical theory, particularly in the Marxist tradition. Critical theory is thus the publishing interest most frequently listed by this group (7 of the 11 activist presses express interest in critical theory in contrast to a total of 4 other presses in the other 2 groups). In keeping with their political goal of reaching a broad spectrum of people, most activist presses prefer research in a form accessible to a general rather than an academic readership.

The second most frequently cited research preference of these presses is women's studies research. They all affirm the importance of feminist work and, without exception, state that they will publish such material. These responses suggest that they perceive feminist theory and the women's movement as integral parts of the process of social change to which they themselves are committed. When we attempt to translate this expression of solidarity into actual publishing practices, however, the prospects suddenly appear less promising. Five activist presses—Pathfinder Press (410 West St., New York, NY 10014), News & Letters (2832 E. Grand Blvd., Rm. 316, Detroit, MI 48211), New England Free Press (60 Union Square, Somerville, MA 02143), Ramparts Press (P.O. Box 10108, Palo Alto, CA 94303), and Challenge Press (1107 Lexington Ave., Dayton, OH 45407)—representing a range of positions within leftist theory and practice, all share the basic view that "we are not researchers but activists" (News & Letters). Their perceived arena is not that of theory and cultural analyses but that of class struggle. And feminism, though a part of this movement, seems to play a subordinate role. Thus, while they lend moral support to "our" struggles, in practice they have time only for "their" own. Challenge Press illustrates this stance. Even though it publishes scholarly research and supports feminism ideologically, it does not publish feminist research. Why? Because, they reply, in their commitment to socioeconomic change they do not rank "the women's struggle . . . among [their] top priorities" and therefore "cannot accept another 'battle to fight.' " The New England Free Press, which prefers research in the form of history, theory, and bibliography and also publishes reprints, is the only one of these five to acknowledge the link between its political activism and that of feminists by expressing interest in feminist critiques of popular culture.

Other activist presses, however, that place greater emphasis on the role of culture in the process of social change and publish in the areas of literature and the arts, are more open to texts with a feminist perspective. West End Press (Box 696, Cambridge, MA 02139) and City Lights Books (261 Columbus Ave., San Francisco, CA 94133) publish creative writings only; both welcome feminist manuscripts. West End, which describes itself as "feminist supporters," publishes neglected works, such as prose writings of working-class women, for the purpose of "aiding scholars in studying feminist material." The attitude of some activist presses toward feminism is rather idiosyncratic. Angel Press (171 Webster St., Monterey, CA 93940), interested in spiritual awareness and in texts that do not conflict with its professed stance of "peaceful coexistence," is eager to receive—within this context— "more provocative feminist and political material." The publishers of Samisdat (Box 231, Richford, VT 05476), who describe themselves as "anarchists/iconoclasts," are basically skeptical of feminist writings, which they suspect may be faddish, even while they admit the theoretical importance of a feminist perspective. They abhor what they call "psychobabble" and academic pedantry and look for the same quality in authors that characterizes their own approach: a radical and self-critical willingness "to carry implications of their work through to all logical conclusions," both in thought and in form.

Press Porcépic, Ltd. (4355 Gordon Head Rd., Victoria, B.C., Canada V8N 3Y6) and House of Anansi Press, Ltd. (35 Britain St., Toronto, Ont., Canada N5A 1R7) effectively use cultural politics for political activism. Canadian presses in every sense of the word, they publish Canadian authors and emphasize a Canadian perspective. Both concentrate mainly on creative writing, but they also favor academic research in the areas of literature and contemporary culture for a college-educated readership. Press Porcépic, interested in Canadian literary criticism, is looking for works that, both formally and ideologically, break out of established patterns to explore "unorthodox critical approaches." Its political-cultural nationalism also determines its approach to women's studies. Since material "based on American experience and data" does not adequately address the situation of Canadian women, it wants a "Canadian women's studies based on Canadian society." House of Anansi, which describes its ideological position as "old Left," is already publishing literature and literary research on and by Canadian women. Since, as it says, "the major Canadian writers are women," its reasoning is compelling; "who," it asked, "would turn away lightly the writer who might be the next Margaret Atwood or Margaret Lawrence?" Because many of its publications are being used as "primary source material in literature, education or social science courses," House of Anansi emphasizes scholarly and artistic excellence.

Scholarly Presses

Most research is sponsored and financed by institutions large enough that their affiliated presses can, therefore, afford to ignore market considerations in their publishing decisions. Independent publishers, however, cannot. As one of the respondents explains: "We are a commercial press. We live by selling our books." Thus, it is not surprising that there are very few small, independent publishers of scholarly research, but seventeen of the presses responding to this survey (37% of total respondents) can be classified as scholarly presses.

These presses speak for and to a select audience of academics and specialists; only a third of the scholarly presses surveyed publish for a general readership. They do not see themselves as doers but as thinkers. Thus, they give highest priority to the dissemination of information (listed by 28%) and emphasize critical thinking and improvement of aesthetic appreciation. A considerable percentage (18%), however, also advocate working for socioeconomic change. The wide range of their goals, as well as the relatively low margin between highest and lowest priorities, indicate that the interests of these presses are as broad as they are dispassionate.

Congruent with this noncommittal stance of openness and impartiality are the responses to my questions concerning their ideological orientation. Like the art presses, most of the scholarly presses either ignore such questions as "irrelevant" or emphatically reject even the suggestion of bias, insisting that "as a scholarly press, we have no political bias" (Press Pacifica). They are, therefore, consistent when they assert, with virtual unanimity, that any manuscript they consider for publication will be judged solely on its scholarly merits. I am surprised that most of the responding scholarly presses favor author-anonymous submission of manuscripts to readers. While this response is in keeping with the general reaction of the surveyed presses to the issue of author-anonymous submission—42% of all respondents will consider or already have such a policy—the scholarly presses voice the strongest support of this practice. One might speculate whether their position reflects their absolute faith in scholarly objectivity or reveals a secret doubt in the impartiality of judgment. Whatever the reasons, their response is encouraging for women scholars.

The scholarly presses do not expect texts themselves to be impartial. While their reactions to texts with explicit political tendencies vary, most of them, like the art presses, claim that no manuscript will be disqualified on the basis of its politics as long as it has intrinsic merit. The same liberal attitude informs their response to feminist scholarship. Not one of the scholarly presses surveyed questions the validity of a feminist perspective or the importance of women's studies as a field of inquiry; they all agree that more feminist research should be published. Nevertheless, merely a third of the presses in this group say that they will actually consider publishing such research. How can one explain this discrepancy?

Exactly half of the responding scholarly presses specialize: they publish research either within a select field (linguistics, film, pedagogy, pop or folk culture) or within a particular historical period or geographic area or they publish a specific kind of text (reference texts, reprints). Their special interests, however, which sometimes include other "minorities," never include women. These specialist presses neither publish nor express interest in research with a focus on women. I suspect that, like some of the art and activist presses, they do not consider a feminist perspective necessary or even important to any scholarly or creative endeavor but instead think of feminism as a narrow and sectarian "study of women." Such a misconception can, of course, be corrected. Therefore, by submitting our manuscripts even to those presses who express a lack of interest in feminism we might allow them to both correct their bias and substantiate their claim that manuscripts will be judged for their scholarship, not for their politics.

Other, less specialized scholarly presses, while receptive to feminist work, hesitate to publish scholarship. Chandler & Sharp Publishers, Inc. (11A Commercial Blvd., Novato, CA 94947), a small publisher of college-level textbooks and nonfiction trade books in literature, contemporary culture, and the humanities, illustrates this problem. They emphasize the importance of women's studies research and even add, "we welcome proposals from and about women." Nevertheless, they discourage the submission of scholarly manuscripts for, without subsidies, they cannot afford to publish texts of a purely scholarly nature.

As I mentioned earlier, however, a third of the responding scholarly presses do present publication possibilities for women's studies research.[4] These five presses publish scholarship in literature and related areas for an academic audience. They insist, without exception, that they will consider manuscripts for publication solely on the basis of scholarly merits. And while they differ in their attention to the ideological aspects of a work, they all demonstrate an active interest in publishing feminist texts. (Although they emphasize research, each of these presses also publishes creative writings.)

Publishing since 1964, Westburg Associates Publishers (1754 Madison St., Fennimore, WI 53809) is the oldest of these presses and the most conservative politically. It emphatically denies that ideological preferences might affect its consideration of a manuscript. Yet in their comments the publishers inadvertently disclose the existence and nature of the preferences they denied: "We are not consciously advocating any sub-cultural movements [and] . . . definitely do not use any material that is derogatory of any peoples . . . or groups," they insist, adding, "Not even white Anglo-Saxon Protestants and male chauvinists!!!" This rather too emphatic protest casts doubt on their claim to complete impartiality. If we take it as a caveat to feminists, we might infer that the more "subdued" our feminism, the more receptive Westburg might be to our work. Westburg's publishing interests extend to all aspects of research in literature (especially comparative literature) and in other humanities disciplines. It prefers interdisciplinary research "written for laymen" [sic].

Founded in 1977, Coda Press (700 Badger Rd., Suite 101, Madison, WI 53713), is the youngest of these five presses, has just begun publishing book-length works, and is projecting an average of four a year. It prefers work that is "progressive"—both formally and politically—but also considers "important, non-politically focussed scholarship." Coda is interested in theory, criticism, and scholarly editions in the areas of literature, contemporary culture, and critical theory. Although the five members of its current editorial board are men, women might be added, I was told, if women's studies manuscripts were under consideration. For the time being, however, Coda is not actively seeking such manuscripts.

The largest press in this group, Three Continents Press (1346 Connecticut Ave., NW, Washington, DC 20036), publishes an average of ten to twelve works a year. Its perspective is clearly defined as "anticolonial, anti-Apartheid, anti-old prejudices of race and sex—and anti-European ethnocentric perspectives." Not only in policy but also in its publishing practice, Three Continents has included a focus on women, particularly third world women, and carries a permanent special listing of texts by and on women in its catalog. This press publishes traditional scholarship, including criticism, biographies, monographs, and bibliographies. It is particularly interested in studies of cross-cultural influences and work on and by neglected writers or groups of writers.

Peregrine Smith, Inc. (P.O. Box 667, 1877 East Gentile St., Layton, UT 84041), the least academically oriented of these scholarly presses, publishes general texts in the area of literature (especially literary history) and fine arts, mainly in the form of anthologies, textbooks, and reprints. Mindful of their "liberal-idealistic Weltanschauung," its editors adopt a consistently neutral stance on all questions addressing their ideological criteria in the evaluation of manuscripts. They profess complete "neutrality" even on the question of whether they consider feminist research a fad or valid scholarship. While this refusal to commit themselves to an opinion makes it difficult to anticipate their actual receptivity, they do express willingness to publish feminist research.

One of the most promising publishers of feminist scholarship among the small presses is York Press (P.O. Box 1172, Fredericton, N.B., Canada, E3B 5C8). Preeminently a scholarly press, York publishes mainly scholarly editions and monographs, preferring research in literature, language, and critical theory. While its editors insist that "scholarly merit, only," is the basis on which a manuscript will be evaluated, they do not discourage politically engaged writings. In fact, they not only express highest esteem for women's studies as a field of inquiry but welcome feminist manuscripts.

I now return to the two questions with which I began. Are small and alternative presses interested in us, and are we interested in them? First, although the publishers I surveyed express mixed reactions to politically engaged, specifically feminist, texts, their overall responsiveness indicates that nonestablishment presses are now receptive to feminist work. The answer to the second question depends on how we, as feminists in academia, define our self-interest and goals. If our primary goals are prestige, academic credentials, or economic security, we would certainly be better served by publishing with a well-known or well-paying academic or commercial press. (And we must recognize that such aspirations, while easily derided as "ignoble," deserve to be taken very seriously. For not only are they essential to building a career and making a living, but the need for and the right to recognition and compensation are issues to which women, often deprived of both, are particularly sensitive.)

Certainly small, alternative presses bring neither fame nor wealth. What they offer us instead is an opportunity to integrate our feminism with our professional work. The problem I raised at the outset was how and where feminist scholars and writers could publish with integrity. Our scholarship and our art cannot be separated from our feminism; whatever we may do, we are feminists. Whether we write as scholars, artists, or activists, we always write as feminists. It is, therefore, not possible to maintain integrity—to remain "whole"—if we are asked to deny part of ourselves in return for publication. Even nonestablished presses, as we have seen, often demand such denials. Ironically, the very presses that, as activists, are most supportive of our feminism seem least receptive to our creative and scholarly endeavors, while the art and scholarly presses, which are interested in us as writers and scholars, tend to be less responsive to us as feminists.

Overall, however, the nonestablishment press offers feminist scholars and creative writers a considerable range of publication possibilities. Pragmatically speaking, it represents a sizable market, for there are many more small presses than large ones; especially "at a time when big publishing finds it necessary to cut back ... the small press flourishes and multiplies" (Foreword, *Alternatives in Print*). The existence of small presses expands our professional options, for even if publishing with a small press does not gain us the same recognition or financial rewards as publishing with a large established press, it can be a means of gaining entry into these more prestigious realms (should that be our goal).

As we pursue our academic or literary careers, however, we must not lose sight of a basic question: For what purpose and for whom are we writing and seeking publication? As feminists our ultimate goal is change, a fundamental change of consciousness and of social structures that will come about only as we express our ideas more fully and freely to a growing number of people. To a significant extent, the nonestablishment press can allow us to do both. It offers us relative freedom to present our message without disguise. Many of the presses I surveyed already support our goals, and most express interest in publishing feminist texts. And, given the basic willingness to cooperate and the liberal political leanings of these presses, even those that are still tentative seem educable to our perspective.

Finally, the nonestablishment press gives us the opportunity to communicate our ideas to a large number of readers we might not otherwise reach, readers who are potential allies and supporters of our work. I believe that while it is important for us as feminists to make our way into the professional realms from which we have been excluded, it is equally important that, as professionals, we do not forget how to speak our ideas in the common language. We can expand the range of feminist activity only by reaching out. Obviously, we do not want to be reduced to a mere (feminist) alternative within a larger (nonestablishment) alternative. We must work to realize our own vision. And, as Charlotte Bunch reminds us, for women the feminist press is not an alternative; it is our future. If we use the opportunities that the nonestablishment press already offers, or promises to provide, we can make it an element in the shaping of that future.

Notes

1. Since the information provided by 1 of the respondents was insufficient, I discuss only 45 (98%) of the responding presses. From the possible publishers of feminist texts, I have selected those few that, in terms of their publishing interests, politics, and relative prestige, are likely to be of greatest interest to academic feminists in modern languages. For a select number of these presses I provide information on manuscript submission and evaluation procedures as well as payment policies (Appendix B).
2. The practice of asking authors to subsidize their books raises the problem of vanity presses. Although the directories I consulted did not distinguish presses on this basis, I attempted to exclude them from the survey, since vanity presses have been disparaged as publishers of academic scholarship. Yet it might be more useful to reevaluate this academic prejudice by exploring its political implications. If we challenge the assumption that only that which is bought and paid for by established institutions can be held in esteem, then paying for our own work can become a political act of self-affirmation. Publishing is neither value-free nor free; we may have to support our work financially in order to sustain our values.
3. Since my survey focuses primarily on the publication of research, the questions discussed in this section asked publishers to describe their responses to feminist *research* only; I did not specifically mention feminist creative writings.
4. Two respondents—Greenwood Press, Inc. (51 Riverside Ave., Westport, CT 06880) and The Shoe String Press, Inc. (P.O. Box 4327, Hamden, CT 06514)—already have special women's studies listings. I will not discuss Greenwood and Shoe String, however, since in their publishing output and international distribution they exceed the bounds of small press publishing.

Appendix A

Project on Research in Women's Studies
MLA Commission on the Status of Women
Survey of Publishers and Small Presses

Questionnaire instructions: For each question, please check as many answers as apply.

1. Name of press:_____

2. Year press began publishing:_____

3. Are you mainly publishers of:

    _____periodical(s)   _____textbooks
    _____reprints   _____anthologies   _____bibliographies
    _____original writings _____scholarly text   _____other (please
                            editions   describe)

4. Number of texts published in average year (not periodicals):_____

5. What kinds of material do you mainly publish:

    _____creative writings _____scholarly   _____both
                            research

6. Do you focus on research in any of the following areas:

    _____literature   _____language   _____critical theory
    _____contemporary   _____fine arts   _____mass media
    culture
    _____minority cultures_____Third World   _____Women's
                                                   Studies
    _____pedagogy   _____interdisci-   _____other (please
                            plinary   describe)

7. Do you favor any of the following kinds of scholarly research:

    _____theory   _____textual   _____history
                            criticism
    _____bibliography   _____monograph   _____other (please
                                                   describe)

8. What mode of research do you prefer:

    _____traditional   _____popularly   _____other (please
    scholarship   accessible   describe)

9. How interested are you in publishing authors in the following categories: Please rank on a scale of   1   2   3

                                    very interested   not interested
   _____local   _____those not tra-
                                     ditionally published

10. Who is your projected readership:
   _____academic   _____non-universi- _____specialists
                               ty   in field
   _____local   _____general   _____other (please
                                            describe)

11. What kinds of texts would you like more of? Less of?

12. How much would you agree/disagree with the following statements: Please rank on a scale of   1   2   3   4   5

                                strongly agree   strongly disagree

   "A text we would consider for publication . . .
   _____ must not have any overt or visible political tendency."
   _____ is judged solely on its scholarly merits regardless of its ideology."
   _____ must have a clear and progressive political stance." (please describe)

13. How would you describe your political or ideological perspective in evaluating materials for publication

14. How much would you agree/disagree with the following opinions about feminist criticism and Women's Studies research:
   Please rank on a scale of   1   2   3   4   5

                       strongly agree   strongly disagree
   _____"It's a fad."
   _____"It's not viable scholarship."
   _____"It's an important field of inquiry."
   _____"There's not enough being published."

15. As a publisher, how would you assess the marketability of Women's Studies research in comparison to other kinds of research:
   _____better   _____about the   _____worse
                             same

16. Would you consider publishing such research: _____ yes
   _____ not now _____ no

17. What effect(s) would you like your press to have on its readership and society:

    _____improve aesthetic   _____further critical thinking
    appreciation

    _____disseminate information _____entertain

    _____promote socio-economic _____other (please describe)
    change

18. How do you prefer authors to submit their work:

    _____query letter   _____query letter and proposal

    _____sample chapter and   _____completed manuscript
    outline

19. Do you accept unsolicited manuscripts: _____yes _____no

20. How many people constitute your regular editorial board:
    How many are women:

21. Who makes editorial decisions: _____editorial collective
    _____editor _____editor(s) and manuscript readers

22. If you use manuscript readers, from which group(s) do you draw them:

    _____in-house   _____non-universi- _____local academic
                             ty

    _____national scholars _____open to sug-
                             gestions by
                             author

23. Would you consider submitting manuscripts anonymously to readers: _____yes _____no _____we already have such a policy

24. What is your payment policy:

25. What is the major source of income of your press:

    _____grant   _____patrons   _____institution
    _____authors   _____editors   _____other (please
                                                     describe)

26. How and where are your publications distributed, promoted, sold:

    _____mail order   _____general book- _____select book-
                             stores   stores

    _____locally   _____nationally

27. Additional comments.

Appendix B

Procedures for manuscript submission and evaluation as well as payment policies of select presses of interest to feminist scholars.

Press	manuscript submission process		manuscript evaluation process			payment policy
	accept unsolicited ms?	preferred submission procedure	press chooses readers	open to author's suggestions	anonymous submission?	
art presses						
1. Bieler	yes	query letter & proposal	"anyone interested"	yes	"unecessary"	copyright/10% royalties
2. Contraband	yes	completed ms. S.A.S.E.	nonuniversity	—	yes	copies
3. Harold House, Publishers	yes	query letter	local academic	—	no	contract negotiated
activist presses						
4. New England Free Press	yes	query letter or/sample chapter & outline	editorial collective	—	yes	in advance
5. West End Press	rarely	query letter & proposal	inhouse & non-university	—	no	copies & 15% of press run
6. Angel Press	yes	sample chapter & outline	inhouse	—	yes	no advance, % of profits
7. Samisdat	yes	query letter	editors	—	no	"we split the press run on books, & whatever authors sell, they keep"

scholarly presses

8. Press Porcépic, Ltd.	yes	sample chapter & outline	editor & selected readers	yes	yes	royalties between 8% and 10%
9. House of Anansi Press, Ltd.	yes	sample chapter & outline	editorial collective	yes	yes	contract negotiated
		would consider co-publishing with American publisher				
10. Chandler & Sharp Publishers, Inc.	yes	query letter & proposal	local & national scholars	yes	yes	[no information]
11. Three Continents Press	rarely	query letter & proposal	local & national scholars	—	no	modest advances, 10% royalties
12. Coda Press, Inc.	no	query letter & proposal	inhouse & local scholars	—	yes	no set policy
13. Peregrine Smith, Inc.	no	query letter	national scholars	—	yes	standard 10%–15% royalties
14. York Press	yes	query letter & proposal	local & national scholars	—	yes	varies
15. Westburg Associates, Publishers	yes	completed manuscript	editor & collective	—	not now	"no payment generally"

Feminist Journals
Writing for a Feminist Future

Charlotte Bunch

The printed word is vital to feminism. Reading and writing were a crucial part of women's efforts for change both in centuries past and throughout the last decade. Lack of access to the printed word characterizes all oppressed groups, and the fight for literacy and control over one's words and thoughts and deeds accompanies all revolutions. The struggle of women is no exception. Only in this century (and then only in some countries and among some classes) have significant numbers of women gained access to the tools of writing Virginia Woolf so thoroughly explored in her essays—literacy, money, admission to the "public world" and its range of experiences, freedom to travel, and space of one's own. Women's efforts to write and to obtain these and other freedoms are one. It is small wonder, then, that writing and publishing are passionate concerns of feminism.

Not insignificantly, the first large purchase of Washington D.C., Women's Liberation in 1968 was a mimeograph machine. We believed, with something akin to religious fervor, that if we could just get copies of "Why Women's Liberation" into enough women's hands, then certainly we could bring female oppression to an end. While that naiveté has given way to a more sophisticated understanding of the complexity of both oppression and social change, a movement was born and the written word remains central to it. Women spread the word about feminism and argue its course in everything from novels to political tracts to personal diaries.

The mimeograph machines have been largely replaced by over two hundred women's periodicals and presses—local, regional, and national—covering a wide array of special interests and general themes in both fiction and nonfiction. I will discuss in depth twenty-one of those publications, feminist journals, national in scope, that seek writers involved in women's studies and feminist scholarship. The selection of these journals is mine alone, but the information about them is based primarily on a questionnaire I sent to each in 1977 inquiring about its editorial perspectives and policies. Since my selection is necessarily limited, the reader should consult the extensive "Directory of Women's Media" published by Media Report to Women,[1] particularly if the journals described here do not seem appropriate for her or his work.

While feminist journals are only one of the places where women can publish, they play an important role in developing feminist writing and in gaining power for women. In the late 1960s, feminists saw the male-dominated media (right, left, and center) diluting articles that we wrote and distorting interviews with us—that is, if they covered us at all. Recognizing the applicability of the maxim "Freedom of the press belongs to those who own the presses," we started our own publications as one way to control our words and their dissemination. Controlling our words corresponds to controlling our bodies, our selves, our work, our lives. Thus, even when there is more receptivity to feminist writing in main-line periodicals, it is still important to create and sustain feminist media as political-cultural-economic institutions maintaining a movement and enhancing women's power.

The importance of feminist media goes beyond just controlling our own institutions. The existence of feminist publications has enabled new work, both that which they publish and often that which appears elsewhere. The feminist media have helped to create a movement and a market for new ideas and new ways of exploring various subjects and questions. This effort is, I believe, their most unacknowledged and most vital function. Those who produce feminist journals do not just passively wait to print already completed work but actively stimulate new work both by asking questions that may not be popular and by printing what is still "unprintable," even unspeakable. The author, editor, and publisher thus engage in a common effort that often involves conflict as well as creativity but that stems from a mutual desire to develop feminist ideas. Such interaction naturally has its problems, but there is still a commonality of purpose and exploration that adds a vital ingredient to the work.

Perhaps the greatest limitation of most feminist journals is their small circulation, with figures generally ranging between two thousand and twenty thousand. If an author seeks an immediate mass audience for a particular piece, a feminist journal may not be the best route. Most circulations are growing, however, and they represent a select audience where the influence of the ideas, as well as the passing around of the journals, often goes far beyond these numbers. The other disadvantage of most feminist journals is that they are understaffed. Often volunteers or low-paid but dedicated individuals do the work of many without sufficient financial backing, which can produce delays in correspondence, in decisions about manuscripts, and sometimes in the publication of the journal itself. I have selected journals with a reputation for reliability, if not always promptness, in their dealings with writers and in their ability to produce their publication.

The journals discussed here are all feminist and interdisciplinary. Some focus on fiction and poetry, others on essays, theory, or scholarship. All welcome submissions from those in languages and literature, as well as from those in other disciplines. Although some journals have overlapping interests and others specifically seek to bridge divisions, they can be categorized roughly into three groups according to their primary emphasis: women's studies and academic, general feminist movement, literary and arts journals.

Most of these journals publish three or four issues a year, but several indicate three or four issues per volume rather than per year; *Atlantis* is biannual and *Makara* is bimonthly. All seek original manuscripts, and most do not reprint already published material except in unusual circumstances. Many print selections from books not yet published. All encourage unsolicited manuscripts (submitted in duplicate and accompanied by a self-addressed, stamped envelope); most also solicit particular writers, especially if publishing around a theme. Few ever commission articles with advance guarantee of publication or payment. In fact, many do not pay fees at all but offer complimentary copies and/or subscriptions to their contributors. *Signs* provides offprints, and *Feminist Studies* hopes to do so in the future.

Generally, feminist journals copyright all material unless the author asks to keep the copyright; several indicated that the copyright automatically reverts to the author on publication. Most grant permission for reprints only with the author's consent and a printed acknowledgment of the journal as the original publisher; if a fee is paid for the reprint (there is great variation about whether a fee is required), most journals divide the money equally with the author. Most of the journals grouped under "Women's Studies" have no graphics except for their covers, but almost all of those in the other two categories have a significant interest in graphics as a central part of their work.

Women's Studies and Academic Journals

In this first grouping of journals primarily focused on women's studies and academic articles, five began in 1972, shortly after women's studies courses had been initiated in a significant number of universities in North America. *Women's Studies Quarterly* (formerly *Women's Studies Newsletter*), published by the Feminist Press (Box 334, Old Westbury, NY 11568), reports on women's studies news and views and on feminist education generally, with a particular focus on what is important to the classroom teacher, whether in schools or colleges. It maintains connections among feminists involved in all educational levels and settings and also serves as the official publication of the National Women's Studies Association (NWSA). What began as a sixteen-page newsletter is now some fifty pages of short articles, reviews of women's studies programs, descriptions of classroom experiences, scholarly bibliographies, job and conference information, essays about particular courses or ideological issues relevant to education, and reports of research. While not thematic, the newsletter sometimes runs a series such as "Evaluating Women's Studies." It seeks material "written in English that is free of jargon and likely to be of interest to some broad spectrum of our readers" and that "is significant for the teacher." Materials are reviewed either by the quarterly working committee or the Advisory Committee of the NWSA; revisions are usually done by the author, but authors do see final copy when edited in-house.

Women's Studies Abstracts, published by Rush Publishing Company (Box 1, Rush, NY 14543), consists primarily of short summaries of material on women appearing in scholarly and feminist publications and lists of additional articles not abstracted. It covers a wide range of topics but aims mainly at those working in the literature of sex roles and characteristics, the status of women, guidance counseling, and teaching. In addition to providing the abstracts and listings, it publishes bibliographic essays, bibliographies, and reviews of the literature in any field concerning women. Politically "feminist—in seeing women as full human beings"—it encourages material from academics and emphasizes the need for thoroughness and accuracy in bibliographic citation. The editor reviews submissions and consults with the author about any changes made.

Resources for Feminist Research, formerly the *Canadian Newsletter of Research on Women* (published at the Ontario Institute for Studies in Education, 252 Bloor St. W., Toronto, Ont., Canada, M5S 1V6), an international periodical of research on women and sex roles, abstracts current Canadian and European and third world work and includes book reviews, bibliographies, a discussion forum, and listings of periodicals and resources from Canada and abroad. (It does not generally incorporate research or conference reports from the United States unless they have a markedly international focus.) The editors are particularly eager to receive short articles for the discussion forum. The publication does not print fiction. Material is reviewed by the entire editorial board; when necessary it is shortened (with marks indicating cuts) but not rewritten, and the author does not see corrected copy in advance. It publishes a Special Publication series—major bibliographies, conference proceedings, edited collections—for which ideas are welcome (send letters of inquiry, not manuscripts, first). Each item is printed in either French or English.

Feminist Studies, an independent journal initiated in New York in 1972, after a brief hiatus in publishing, began an association (but not a merger) with the University of Maryland in 1977 (Women's Studies Program, Univ. of Maryland, College Park 20742). Its expanded board sees women "at a new intellectual and political juncture" and believes:

> Feminist thought represents a revolution in consciousness, social forms, and political struggles. Placing the condition of women, and sex as a category of analysis, at the center of inquiry and action has the potential dramatically to reshape the questions, theories, contours, and meanings of intellectual and social life.

It welcomes critical, scholarly, and speculative essays, reviews, conversations, and creative work (poetry and art but not fiction) that assume this perspective and contribute to feminist theory and consciousness. The members of the board represent diverse political perspectives; articles are reviewed by at least two of its editors and chosen collectively. Editors work closely with an author on major rewrites; the author sees final page proofs.

Women's Studies: An Interdisciplinary Journal, published by Gordon and Breach Science Publishers (1 Park Ave., New York, NY 10016; editorial office: Wendy Martin, Dept. of English, Queens Coll., City Univ. of New York, Flushing, NY 11367) and the last of the journals begun in 1972, provides a forum for presenting scholarship and criticism about women in literature, history, art, sociology, law, political science, economics, anthropology, and the sciences. It also publishes poetry, short fiction, and reviews of books and films. Special thematic issues, such as Rites of Passage of American Women, are sometimes published, often under the direction of guest editors. The editors have no particular political orientation; they are "interested in well-written, carefully researched articles in the field of feminist criticism." The editors and the editorial board review articles but do not provide a report of the reasons for rejection. While the authors may be asked to make specific changes and correct final proofs, neither authors nor editors do major rewrites of articles.

Another cluster of women's studies journals began in 1974–75. The first of these was the *University of Michigan Papers in Women's Studies,* published in nine issues from 1975 to 1978 and containing articles in a variety of disciplines. Now known as the Michigan Occasional Papers Series (354 Lorch Hall, Ann Arbor, MI 48109), the twenty titles thus far include monographs, articles, bibliography, and women's studies research. The editors seek papers with provocative ideas and new approaches, often difficult to publish in traditional disciplinary journals. Suggestions for revision and occasionally rewrites are sent to authors, who must return the manuscript in "copy-ready form."

Signs: Journal of Women in Culture and Society, published by the University of Chicago Press (Editorial office: Center for Research on Women, Stanford Univ., Stanford, CA 94305), publishes new scholarship from any discipline and any country "about women, sex roles, the social institutions in which the sexes have participated, and the culture men and women have inherited, inhabited, and created." *Signs* looks for new data, new theories, and new ways of looking at women's lives and has as its only political bias "a prejudice against articles that are blatantly sexist." In literature, the editors prefer articles that discuss an author's work in its entirety or consider more than one author. It does not publish fiction or poetry. Two issues a year of this regular quarterly have a theme, such as Women and Religion. Only review essays are solicited, and all articles are read by two people in the office; articles under serious consideration are sent author-anonymously to referees in the field. (Submissions should have the author's name on the title page only.) Major rewrites are done in consultation with the author, who sees the final version. It can take four to six months to complete the refereeing procedure, and the time between acceptance and publication runs from one year to eighteen months.

Atlantis: A Women's Studies Journal (Mt. St. Vincent Univ., 166 Bedford Highway, Halifax, N.S., Canada B3M 2J6) is an interdisciplinary journal devoted to critical and creative writing (in English or French) on the topic of women. Mostly Canadian in origin and content, the twelve issues published to date include major scholarly papers, book and film reviews, review essays, conference and research reports, poetry, some fiction, comments and replies, and visual arts. The editorial board welcomes submissions, not more than ten thousand words in length, embodying all points of view on women's studies. Where major rewrites or important editorial changes are made, the author is consulted.

Frontiers: A Journal of Women's Studies, published in association with the Women's Studies Program at the University of Colorado (Hillside Court 104, Boulder, CO 80309) and now in its sixth volume, aims at "bridging the gap between university and community women." It accepts scholarly articles in any discipline, essays concerning the problems of women in the "real world," reviews, exceptional creative work, criticism, rejoinders, informal short notes about personal experiences and insights, and responses to work published. While not thematic, each issue does have a cluster of articles around a topic such as

Woman as Victim. Committed to radical feminism and the women's movement, its editors look for the "accessibility" of work to nonacademic women as well as its import to women scholars. They desire a variety of points of view in the journal, encourage collaborative as well as interdisciplinary work, and review material through the editorial collective and outside referees. Revisions are sometimes requested from authors and all rewrites are subject to author's approval; the editors note that "the process of publication is as important as the actual printing and distribution of journals, and thus, we have always worked very closely with our authors."

Among the many other academic journals are the following: *Feminist Issues* (editorial office: 2948 Hillegass, Berkeley, CA 94705), an English-language edition of the French feminist journal *Questions Feministes*, publishes translations of previously printed French feminist articles as well as "theoretical work by English-speaking feminists." This journal, started in the summer of 1980, will help to connect feminists working in France and the United States. *Women and Literature* (editorial office: Janet Todd, Dept. of English, Douglass Coll., Rutgers Univ., New Brunswick, NJ 08903), formerly a quarterly, began an annual format in 1980. Each volume of the new series will contain several articles that "focus on a specific theme in literary or artistic criticism, the first one exploring the question of gender and literary voice." *Women's Studies International Quarterly* (regional associate editor: Cheris Kramar, Univ. of Illinois, 224 Lincoln Hall, Urbana 61801), now in its fourth volume, is devoted to the "rapid dissemination" of scholarship and criticism in anthropology, archaeology, art, communications, economics, education, health, history, law, linguistics, literature, the media, philosophy, political science, psychology, religion, science, sociology, and urban studies. The editors invite articles, information, and material "that might be appropriately published under the headings of research, review and women's studies," and manuscripts are to be submitted with the author's name on a separate title page only.

General Feminist Movement Journals

The following journals have a general feminist orientation and do not usually address women's studies specifically, but they do have considerable relevance to the area. Whereas some of the journals in the first group are published by universities or other institutions, all those in this group and the third group are published independently by the women who produce them. *Women: A Journal of Liberation* (3028 Greenmount Ave., Baltimore, MD 21218), one of the first feminist journals, begun in 1969, sees itself as "a tool for the women's move-

ment, which tries to embody, in form and content, the basic principles
of that movement: an identification with all women, a non-hierarchical
structure, and an overview of social forces focused on concrete, personal accounts of how those forces affect women's lives and how wom-
en affect them." Socialist-feminist in political perspective, it seeks to
introduce women to the women's movement and to promote dialogue
among women working for change. Each issue is organized around a
theme, such as Women Alone, and includes articles (usually short), fiction, poetry, reviews, artwork, and photography. The collective especially seeks submissions that women who may not have an academic
background or who may not participate in the movement will find
readable. The author and editor work together, but the author usually
does any rewriting. The journal tries to include the work of women
with a wide variety of experiences, backgrounds, and life-styles and to
distribute the magazines as widely and as cheaply as possible.

Second Wave (Box 344, Cambridge A., Cambridge, MA 02139),
billed as "a magazine of the new feminism," began in 1971. The editors see themselves as striving to publish a broad-based journal that is
visually and intellectually accessible to many women. While the magazine does not have a "correct line," the material it prints must be
"radical feminist and readable—that is, not pseudo-intellectual or
overly academic." It includes nonfiction essays, fiction, poetry, reviews, graphics, and photography. The review process involves collective evaluation, and the time between receipt of material and
publication is lengthy. Material is often strenuously edited or returned
to the author for work, but the editors seldom rewrite it. The *Second
Wave* postscript reads: "We try to inhabit that improbable realm between the professional and the slick, theory and tedium, art and polemic, the visionary and the inaccessible. We may not always succeed,
but the effort is made and the need acknowledged."

Quest: A Feminist Quarterly (Box 9086, Washington, DC 20003), begun in 1974, seeks a synthesis of feminist writing that brings together
the best of theoretical and practical approaches in a journal of feminist
ideas and analysis. Each issue covers a theme in depth, such as Money,
Fame, and Power, and once a year the journal publishes an open forum issue with no theme. *Quest* focuses on political analysis and includes articles, interviews, book or movie review essays, graphic
illustrations, responses to previous articles, organizers' dialogue on
movement problems and successes. Radical feminist in orientation, it
explores differences and similarities in various ideologies and strate-
gies in an effort both to evaluate past practice and to propel feminism
forward. Submissions are read by at least two editors, and decisions
about what to publish are made jointly by the staff and a development
committee created around each theme. Major rewrites are frequently

done but with final approval given to the author. *Quest*'s emphasis in evaluation and editing is on clarity, relevance both to the particular theme and to political strategy, and originality of ideas or research.

Makara Magazine (1011 Commercial Dr., Vancouver, B.C., Canada V5L 3X1) was started in 1975 in order to present a feminist perspective on any aspect of Canadian society in a way that makes this point of view accessible to the general public. It features articles, interviews, photos and art portfolios, fiction, poetry, and features for and by children. Some issues are organized around themes, such as Myths and Symbols. The editors are looking for work produced in Canada or about Canada that makes a positive contribution to changing society and has a minimum of jargon. Authors collaborate in editing and see all corrected copy. *Makara* receives more fiction and poetry than it can use, but it desires more research articles in any field and hopes that women academics will put their work forward more aggressively.

Finally, there are special-interest feminist magazines not discussed in-depth here that might welcome academic articles in their areas of concern; for example: *Aegis: Magazine on Ending Violence against Women* (Feminist Alliance against Rape and National Communications Network, Box 21033, Washington, DC 20009), a bimonthly magazine sharing information and ideas among antirape organizers internationally; *Connexions: An International Women's Quarterly* (People's Translation Service, 4228 Telegraph Ave., Oakland, CA 94609), a journal of English translations of articles by, for and about women in all parts of the world; *ISIS International Bulletin* (C.P. 50 [Cornavin], 1211 Geneva 2, Switzerland), a quarterly that prints theoretical and practical information and documentation from the women's movement around the world, in both English and Spanish; *WIN News* (187 Grant St., Lexington, MA 02173), a quarterly containing international news of women, arranged by departments—health, publications and media, United Nations, development, international reports, violence, environment, human rights, genital and sexual mutilation; *Womanspirit* (Box 263, Wolf Creek, OR 97497), a quarterly journal for consciousness raising in the sphere of women's inner (spiritual) experience and in the evolution of women's new culture.

Literary and Arts Journals

Except for *13th Moon*, all the literary and arts journals that responded to my questionnaire were founded in 1976 or 1977. *13th Moon* (Drawer F, Inwood Sta., New York, NY 10034) was begun in 1973 in order to provide a forum for the diversity of literature being produced by women. Its editors hope that "by exploring the special relationship women have to themselves and to the world, the journal will discover literature that is unique, that is female, that is ours." Nonthematic, it has primarily published poetry, fiction, graphics, and reviews, but it would like to include more feminist and/or lesbian criticism, research on lesser-known women writers, papers on sexism in language, and translations. It is open to anything that is well-written, interesting, and germane to a literary magazine publishing women exclusively. Work is not judged on its political merits, and the editors try to "publish the best literary magazine," which includes a broad, balanced sampling in each issue. Poets are informed of any proposed changes, and other writers are consulted on any major changes; however, most of the material that is selected does not require much editing.

Sibyl-Child (Box 1773, Hyattsville, MD 20788) is a women's art and culture journal whose purpose is to present fiction, poetry, articles, reviews, interviews, photographs, and graphics by women based on a "progressive" political perspective. It welcomes critical articles commenting on aspects of our society and prints any good material that falls within its purpose as an arts and culture journal. Sometimes *Sibyl-Child* has themes, such as Women: Their Art, Their Image, focusing on interviews with women artists, directors, and editors. The editors of this journal try to respond to all submissions with personal comments, and authors see corrected copy when any rewriting is done.

Sinister Wisdom (P.O. Box 660, Amherst, MA 01004) is a lesbian-feminist journal of art, language, and politics, committed to dialogue beyond all assumed or existing boundaries. One of the eighteen issues published to date presents the theme Lesbian Writing and Publishing, but issues include all forms of writing—poetry, fiction, letters, essays, biography, and plays. *Sinister Wisdom*'s former editors declare:

> [we] want to publish work that uncovers and speaks out of all aspects of Lesbian experience . . . and that analyzes the various devious ways in which patriarchal language and institutions operate. We're extremely eager for substantial research and theory, but prefer that it be done with a sense of speaking directly to our readers. . . .We have never required that contributors be Lesbian-identified—only that they be comfortable enough with the magazine to want to be published in it without a disclaimer revealing their "true" orientations.

No material is cut or revised without the author's permission.

Heresies: A Feminist Publication on Art and Politics (Heresies Collective, Inc., 225 Lafayette St., New York, NY 10012), begun in 1977, is an idea-oriented journal devoted to the examination of art and politics from a feminist perspective. It hopes to stimulate dialogue around radical political and aesthetic theory, encourage the writing of the history of *Femina sapiens,* and generate new creative energies among women. Each issue deals with a theme, such as Women and Violence, and a different editorial collective created for each theme solicits and reviews material. Political perspectives within the ongoing collective vary; any submissions to the journal will be considered, except for monographs on living artists. Editing is done primarily because of space limitations (articles tend to be short); little rewriting is done, although edited versions must have the author's approval. *Heresies* views feminism as process and change and hopes that through diversity and dialogue it can broaden the definition and function of art.

Conditions (Box 56, Van Brunt Sta., Brooklyn, NY 11215), also begun in 1977, is a magazine of writing by women and especially by lesbians. It is interested in poetry, short fiction, excerpts from novels, drama, journal entries, translations, excerpts from correspondence, interviews, reviews, and critical articles on the women's and lesbian movements and institutions, on issues involving race, class, and age, and on aspects of lesbian relationships. The collective editorial process emphasizes work in a variety of styles by both published and unpublished writers from many different backgrounds. The editors do not have to agree with the author's point of view to publish the work; when rewriting is necessary, the editors work closely with authors, who must consent to any changes.

Some other journals in the arts and literature include *Azalea: A Magazine by and for Third World Lesbians* (306 Lafayette Ave., Brooklyn, NY 11238), a publication of thoughts and feelings, expressed primarily in fiction and poetry but including some nonfiction prose; *Black Maria* (P.O. Box 25187, Chicago, IL 60625), a journal of women's art and politics published collectively and including essays about current issues in the women's movement, fiction, poetry, photographs, pen-and-ink work; *Moving Out: Feminist Literary and Arts Journal* (4866 Third St., Rm. 306, Wayne State Univ., Detroit, MI 48202), a journal of poetry, fiction, drama, artwork, and resources published twice a year by a collective of women who recognize the need for a medium through which women can share ideas and experiences; *Primavera: A Magazine of Writing and Artwork by Women* (Univ. of Chicago Feminist Organization, 1212 E. 59th St., Chicago, IL 60637), a compendium of prose, poetry, graphics, and photographs by women; *Room of One's Own* (P.O. Box 46160, Sta. G, Vancouver, B.C., Canada V6R 4G5), a feminist literary quarterly featuring original prose, poetry, essays, and reviews by both new and published writers; *Women Artists News* (Midmarch Associates, P.O. Box 3304, Grand Central Sta., New York, NY 10017), a publication devoted to women in the visual arts that appears ten months of the year. Some newer journals that combine the arts and literature with scholarship, criticism, personal, and movement writing include *Common Lives Lesbian Lives* (P.O.

Box 1553, Iowa City, IA 52244), which publishes "history, oral history, biography, autobiography, correspondence, fiction, fantasy, theory, analysis, performed arts and reviews"; *Feminary* (P.O. Box 954, Chapel Hill, NC 27514), which publishes "articles, personal narratives, journal excerpts, letters, short fiction, poetry, drawings, photographs"; *Maenad* (P.O. Box 738, Gloucester, MA 01930), which publishes factual and theoretical articles, biography and history, fiction, reviews, criticism, and bibliographies, preferably concerning "controversial feminist and radical feminist ideas and theories."

As one who has worked with feminist publications for some time, as both an editor and a writer, I have a few practical suggestions for writers. Submit your work to only one publication at a time. Often women who are anxious to be published send the same material to more than one journal, creating confusion, anger, and even legal problems. If the timeliness of a topic requires that you send your manuscript to more than one publication simultaneously, then tell each journal what you are doing and notify the other journals who have your work if one of them accepts it. When you send a manuscript to a journal, enclose both a self-addressed, stamped envelope for its return and a stamped, self-addressed postcard requesting immediate notification of receipt of your submission (things do get lost in the mail) and an estimate of how long the procedure for review will take. Allow enough review time for what is often a group decision. If the time that a journal holds your work exceeds the estimate given or goes beyond six months, then inquire in writing about what is happening with your material and, unless the journal expects to print it, request it back so that you can submit it elsewhere. When you send a journal two copies of your manuscript, be sure to keep a copy for yourself. If you want feedback as to why a submission has been rejected or suggestions of other places to send it, ask for that information specifically. In short, use common sense. Do not be awed by the publishing procedure but do have patience, since the staffs of most feminist journals are overworked. State your needs and plans in a firm, sympathetic, and straightforward manner, expect and ask for the same in return, and publishing with a feminist journal should be a rewarding experience.

Note

1. "Directory of Women's Media," first published in January 1975 and updated yearly by *Media Report to Women,* 3306 Ross Pl., NW, Washington, DC 20008, available for $8. Several of the short descriptions of publications listed at the end of each section were drawn primarily from this valuable directory.

Other Words
Alternative Publishing Outlets
for Women Writers

Ann Romines and Thomazine W. Shanahan

While we were graduate students in women's studies and literature, the pressing question whenever three or four of us were together was "But how do we get published?" What we usually meant was how do we get published in *Signs* or in other scholarly journals. Our vision encompassed no less than a twenty-page article with forty-seven footnotes. In our eagerness to be recognized as credentialed professionals, we tended to see anything less than a book version of our thesis or an article in the *Massachusetts Review* as trifling.

Time and experience have taught most of us otherwise. What we have learned is not so much to lower our sights as to broaden them. Once we forgot the notion that "getting published" referred only to full-length scholarly articles, we discovered that there are hundreds of publications—newsletters, bulletins, newspapers, and magazines—where women's studies scholars can send short articles, profiles, and book reviews. Seeking such outlets broadens our purpose as well, for when we share our research or our experience with an audience outside the academic world, we are acting in a practical, political way to advance the feminist purposes of women's studies.

The best-known sourcebook for identifying such publications, *Writer's Market* (ed. Bruce Joel Hillman [Cincinnati: Writer's Digest, 1978]), contains listings of university presses, commercial publishers, radio and television stations, and an array of magazines—trade, pulp, slick, comic, adventure, women's, sports, literary, historical, black, political, alternative, and many others. Additional useful guides, somewhat less known, are *Ulrich's International Periodicals Directory* (New York: Bowker, 1978), *Magazines for Libraries* (ed. Bill Katz and Berry G. Richards, 3rd ed. [New York: Bowker, 1978]), and *Standard Periodical Directory* (6th ed. [New York: Oxbridge Communications, 1978]), which claims to be the most comprehensive of the three. *Magazines for Libraries*, unlike the others, is thoroughly and helpfully annotated. The standard *Ayer Directory of Publications* (Philadelphia: Ayer), published annually, lists newspapers and magazines by state and town and academic journals by institution.

Probably the first outlets considered by most women's studies scholars are academic publications. They encompass, as well as the standard scholarly journals of the disciplines, a variety of newsletters, bulletins, and magazines published by honorary, professional, and independent organizations and by colleges and universities. The American Association of University Professors, for instance, circulates two magazines that print articles on academic issues: *Academe* (8 issues per year; Suite 500, 1 DuPont Circle, Washington, DC 20036) and the quarterly *AAUP Bulletin* (same address). A recent *Bulletin* included two articles especially close to many women academics' interests: "Academic Recommendations: Males and Females as Judges and Judged" and "Who Is Part-time in Academe?" Contributors are AAUP members. Another campus organization, Phi Beta Kappa (118 Q St., NW, Washington, DC 20009) publishes a prestigious quarterly, the *American Scholar,* which includes articles from all disciplines, as well as poetry and often lengthy and speculative review essays. One issue contains a reappraisal by Ellen Moers, "The Fraternal George Sand," but women writers and women's issues seem generally underrepresented.

Women's issues are the specific concern of *On Campus with Women* (Association of American Colleges, 1818 R St., NW, Washington, DC 20009). This quarterly newsletter, published by the privately funded Project on the Status and Education of Women, consists of unsigned summary accounts of the many developments, studies, laws, programs, and publications concerning women and higher education. Some of the writing is done by undergraduates, graduate students, or law student interns, who may receive academic credit for their work. (Write the address above for information on the internship program.) One intern, for example, was substantially responsible for a recent special report distributed by the Project on Women, "The Problem of Rape on Campus."

The publications of another academic organization, the American Association of University Women, reach a large female audience on and off campuses. A quarterly state *Bulletin,* in newsletter form, publishes brief articles on local and national organization news and news of women's political candidacies and issues. The current Missouri *Bulletin* includes short signed items by members on an Adult Abuse Bill before the state legislature and on a university program training women in feeder-pig production. A substantial bimonthly magazine, *Graduate Woman* (2401 Virginia Ave., NW, Washington, DC 20037), "carefully considers" unsolicited manuscripts from AAUW members. Articles, brief news items, and books reviewed deal with national and international women's issues. The cover article for a recent issue profiles a woman anthropology student who established an important museum of American Indian art. Another article, by a historian, analyzes the developments that led, in seventeenth-century Italy, to the first awarding of a university degree to a woman.

The weekly newspaper for academics, the *Chronicle of Higher Education* (1717 Massachusetts Ave., NW, Washington, DC 20036), accepts twelve to fifteen unsolicited articles a year, which the editors hope will "clearly and forcefully" examine a "timely topic which we have not dealt with before." The *Chronicle*'s Point of View columns concentrate on academic experience, but female views and issues often seem to receive short shrift, so a feminist contribution—such as Arlene Okerlund's "Will Women's Studies Survive?" (16 April 1979)—should prove "timely." The *Chronicle* also prints lengthy and substantive letters, in which readers might raise issues to which the paper does not always appear receptive in its editorial departments. Another academic publication, the newsletter *NEA Advocate* (published 8 times a year by National Education Association, 1201 Sixteenth St., NW, Washington, DC 20036), also publishes letters in Faculty Forum and invites readers to use the space "to express opinions and share information with their colleagues . . . across the country."

Publications from your own college or university, past or present, may be eager to receive contributions from you. Alumni magazines, for example, regularly print reviews, columns, and short profiles and often welcome articles on women who were directly or indirectly a part of the institutional history, on innovative research and teaching programs, and on conferences. Many such magazines, in short supply of paid writing staff, solicit well-written articles by alumni, faculty, students, and community members. A small midwestern alumni bulletin recently included a profile-interview with a former student in her eighties, who recalled treatment of women during the college's early days. A California magazine reported research on the history of contraceptive techniques among American women, and an urban university newsletter featured an article on local women's contributions to early city planning.

Most larger colleges and universities also produce magazines for the on-campus community of current students, teachers, and administrators. Some, like George Washington University's *GW Forum,* focus on a specific theme in each issue. An issue on work included essays and interviews that touched on a number of women's issues. Other magazines, like the University of Cincinnati's *Clifton,* cover a wide range of topics in each issue. In fall 1978, *Clifton* published a lengthy evaluation of the university's affirmative action progress and a study of Cincinnati's reaction to a local feminist musician. Such magazines usually encourage contributions, as do university newspapers, which seem perennially in need of writers, particularly for their arts sections.

On-campus newsletters are yet another possibility. Your own department may have a newsletter that publishes news, summaries, and excerpts of current faculty and student work. Most women's studies departments also circulate newsletters through the university and often to women's studies on other campuses as well. Such newsletters may include news of local events and fellowships, abstracts of current publications, and short articles by students and faculty members currently doing work on women's topics. The editor of one university newsletter recently told us that she, like every other editor she knows, is constantly looking for brief, incisive reviews of books related to women's studies.

Within the academic field of languages and literatures, many newsletters are published by professional associations, independent editors, and women's groups. *MLA Newsletter* (62 Fifth Ave., New York, NY 10011), sent to the MLA's membership four times per year, includes letters to the editor, announcements, and short pieces on matters of professional and scholarly concern. The six regional MLA associations also publish newsletters and bulletins that report their memberships' activities and reprint papers delivered at regional meetings.

The Women's Caucus of the Modern Languages, like many other disciplinary caucuses of women, publishes a quarterly newsletter, *Concerns* (ed. Patricia A. Quinn, 68 Murray St., Binghamton, NY 13905). A cornucopia of short writings, each issue offers news of women's programming and politics for MLA national and regional meetings, brief descriptions of women's studies conferences and programs, calls for papers, announcements of jobs, appointments, and awards, reports of discrimination grievances, legal proceedings, and harassments, notices of new publications, resource lists (a recent issue listed feminist bookstores throughout the country), and a section on research in progress.

A number of newsletters concentrate on a single woman writer; they may contain bibliographic and biographical studies, as well as brief articles, notes, letters, and calls for papers that often do not appear in other feminist publications. A recent number of the *Eudora Welty Newsletter* (Dept. of English, Univ. of Toledo, Toledo, OH

43606) included "Blurbs: Welty on Elizabeth Spencer," tracing Welty's comments on another woman novelist. Representative contributions to the *Doris Lessing Newsletter* (c/o Dee Seligman, 35 Prospect St., Sherburn, MA 01770) have been "Olive Schreiner: Touchstone for Lessing" and an essay comparing a recent traveler's impressions of Rhodesia with the Africa of Lessing's fiction. Other such single-focus newsletters are *George Sand Newsletter* (3 issues per year; Hofstra Univ., Hempstead, NY 11550); *Marianne Moore Newsletter* (biannual, encourages contributions "on all aspects of Marianne Moore and her work, up to 750 words"; 2010 Delancey Pl., Philadelphia, PA 19103), *Ellen Glasgow Newsletter* (biannual; Edgar E. MacDonald, Box 565, Ashland, VA 23005), and *Under the Sign of Pisces: Anaïs Nin and Her Circle* (interviews, letters, criticism, and bibliography on Nin and members of her circle who appear in the diaries; 1858 Neil Ave., Columbus, OH 43210).

Some of these single-author newsletters are listed in the directories mentioned at the beginning of this article, but no directory provides a comprehensive list. *Magazines for Libraries* suggests the periodical *Serials Review* (Pierian Press, P.O. Box 1808, Ann Arbor, MI 48106) as a continuing source for detailed critical reviews of new newsletters, as well as Judith Farley's article, "Author, Author," in *LC Information Bulletin* (2 Dec. 1977, pp. 800–02). Writers who are interested in a particular literary figure should also remember the larger, better-known single-author periodicals, like the semiannual *Emily Dickinson Bulletin* (Higginson Press, 4508 38th St., Brentwood, MD 20722) and *Virginia Woolf Quarterly* (Aeolian Press, 6762 Cibola Rd., San Diego, CA 92120). *Virginia Woolf Miscellany* publishes excellent reviews of books and articles on Woolf, as well as short pieces and notes (Sonoma State Univ., Rohnert Park, CA 94928). An annual *Flannery O'Connor Bulletin* (Georgia Coll., Milledgeville, GA 31061) features five or six longer articles on O'Connor, as well as book reviews and briefer comments and announcements. Biographical, bibliographic, and critical articles on Elizabeth Barrett Browning and on "other literary and artistic figures" associated with the Brownings are solicited by the annual *Browning Institute Studies* (Dept. of English, Univ. of Maryland, College Park 20742).

Other disciplines, especially history, philosophy, the arts, psychology, and education, produce publications that may welcome short reviews, profiles, and articles on women whose achievements have spanned the disciplines. Colleagues may suggest pertinent publications in their fields. For example, a feminist historian referred us to *CCWHP Newsletter,* sponsored by the Coordinating Committee for Women in the Historical Profession, which prints announcements, news items, and letters concerning women historians. She also recom-

mended *Conference Group in Women's History Newsletter,* which
publishes professional news, queries, reports on research in progress,
and brief bibliographic essays surveying work on women's history,
such as "Women in South Asia: Initial Explorations" and "The Histori-
ography of Canadian Women's History." (Both historians' newsletters
may be reached through Anita Rapove, Mounted Rt. 8, Box 373, Platts-
burgh, NY 12901.) Activities of the College Art Association are reported in the lively and substantial *Women Artists Newsletter* (Box 3304,
Grand Central Sta., New York NY 10017), which features reviews of
books and exhibits, news on women artists, and interviews, most of
which come from feminist scholars. Women sociologists contribute articles on research and teaching projects to *SWS Newsletter* (Sociologists
for Women in Society, Schlesinger Library, Radcliffe Coll., 3 James St.,
Cambridge, MA 02138); psychologists publish *Psychology of Women:
Division 35 Newsletter* (American Psychological Association, c/o Virginia E. O'Leary; 1200 Seventeenth St., NW, Washington, DC 20036).

Women's studies scholars produce the well-known and growing
Women's Studies Quarterly (Feminist Press, Box 334, Old Westbury,
NY 11568), the official publication of the National Women's Studies Association. The editorial committee considers unsolicited articles of
about 2,400 words that "concentrate on practical and theoretical issues
involved in the teaching . . . development, and administration of wom-
en's studies programs, and other matters of particular interest to feminist educators on all levels and in all settings." Recent issues have
included a bibliography on women in Renaissance literature, an essay
on white women teaching black women writers, "Teaching about the
History of Women in Western Music," "Finding and Studying Lesbian
Culture," and contrasting student and administrative evaluations of a
particular university's women's studies program. Editor Shirley Frank
also suggests that short "informational notes" be sent to Newsbriefs.
Regional divisions of NWSA also produce smaller newsletters. *North
Central Newsletter,* for example, runs regional news of work in progress and solicits brief reviews of books and films for its Women's Stud-
ies Resources section (Women's Studies, Indiana Univ., Memorial Hall
East 128, Bloomington 47401).

Women scholars should also consider submitting their work to the
many women-oriented publications produced in the world outside academe. For instance, professional women's groups publish in great volume. A roster of ninety-six organizations, ranging from the American
Association of Women in Community and Junior Colleges to the Association of American Dentists, is available from the American Association of University Women (2401 Virginia Ave., NW, Washington, DC
20037). Most publish at least newsletters with book-review sections;
some produce magazines or journals as well. The *Journal of the Na-*

tional Association for Women Deans, Administrators, and Counselors (editor changes from issue to issue; see current issue for name and address), for example, publishes articles of 2,500–3,000 words. A recent copy includes "Ethnic Minority Feminism," a symposium, and articles entitled "Women's Studies Emerging" and "Debunking the Myths of Affirmative Action." *National Business Woman,* a magazine of the National Federation of Business and Professional Women's Clubs (2012 Massachusetts Ave., NW, Washington, DC 20036), prints briefer articles that aim to interest women in a wide variety of fields, such as "How Women Fared in the November Elections." A bimonthly newsletter, *Women in Libraries* (c/o Kay Kassell, Bethlehem Public Library, Delmar, NY 12054) consists of six to ten pages of news about jobs, meetings, and conferences for women librarians, as well as notes on books, films, and records of special interest to women.

A new professional organization, Feminist Writers Guild, is "a service group and a political body . . . open to any woman who takes her writing seriously." The guild publishes a quarterly national newsletter (P.O. Box 9396, Berkeley, CA 94709) that, although largely devoted to national and local organization news, includes calls for feminist articles. A recent issue reports that the New York City chapter of the guild is producing a bimonthly supplement to *New Women's Times* "on literature and the arts. Those who wish to review books should send a letter explaining their interest, a sample of their work, and a SASE to *The Feminist Review*" (682 Broadway, New York, NY 10012). Books for review are chosen by or assigned to reviewers; the editors are "also interested in having pieces about previously published works that have been either neglected or trashed in the male press."

Women's political groups also publish newsletters, newspapers, and small magazines. *National NOW Times* (425 13th St., NW, Washington, DC 20004), the official monthly newspaper of the National Organization for Women, runs articles by members that "concern either NOW activities or issues of interest to the women's movement." Such articles survey and analyze ERA and legislative progress or other political issues, as in "Women's Needs Ignored in 1980 Budget"; other articles have considered feminist history and have profiled feminists (Alice Paul, e.g.). An Opinion page has included a piece entitled "On Iranian Women" and "Woman as Witch: Can Magic Be Blamed for Capitalism?" Local NOW organizations may also publish newsletters; *Cincinnati NOW,* for instance, features "news and comments" and briefly reviews publications of political interest to local women.

Another political group, the National Women's Political Caucus, produces *Women's Political Times* (1411 K St., NW, Washington, DC 20005), a bimonthly newsletter that considers unsolicited articles (by line by request) that, according to an editor, "promote the feminist perspective in politics and the general political education of American women . . . and identify and articulate issues of significant political implication for women." Recent issues surveyed federal judgeship appointments, women's relation to social security, implications of the Abzug firing, and changes in alimony policy. Another such newsletter, *Women's Agenda* (monthly; 370 Lexington Ave., New York, NY 10017), sponsored by Women's Action Alliance, prints brief reports on current women's issues, coverage of women's events, and signed reviews of a wide variety of women-oriented books on subjects ranging from menopause to economic power.

Other organizational newsletters include *YWCA Interchange* (bimonthly; 600 Lexington Ave., New York, NY 10022), which, though largely devoted to YWCA news and policy, prints occasional book reviews. And the Gray Panthers, a woman-founded political group whose membership includes women and men, also publishes a bimonthly newsletter, *Gray Panther Network: Age and Youth in Action* (3700 Chestnut St., Philadelphia, PA 19104). Christina Long, editor, invites contributions from Panthers and non-Panthers "across the country." The current issue includes "Middle-Age Spread," a half-page essay on men's and women's differing attitude toward their own middle age; brief reviews of books related to aging, including May Sarton's most recent novel; and a dialogue between Panthers and a woman nursing-home administrator. A regular column, "Approaches to Ageing," requests contributions describing "feelings, personal experiences, and beliefs about ageing."

Another group of independent publications, often among the most eager to receive contributions from feminist writers, includes those that are feminist and cultural, if not strictly academic, in orientation. For example, *Moving Out* (biannual; 4866 Third, Wayne State Univ., Detroit, MI 48202) prides itself on being "open to new contributors" of essays, criticism, poetry, fiction, reviews (books, records, art), photographs, art, and interviews. Editor Margaret Kaminski says, "frequently we publish women who have never sent out work or been published before. . . . we try not to be snobbish and look for a university logo at the top of a cover letter! In fact, we tend to avoid the overly-academic type of paper. . . .We like work which illustrates womanlife, or has some new viewpoint using women's aesthetic." A list of *Moving Out*'s contributors includes such names as Adrienne Rich, Audre Lord, Robin Morgan, and Marge Piercy, as well as lesser-known contributors. Recent essays have considered "The Married Woman Artist," "The Post-Abortion Experience: Relief or Guilt?" "Diane Arbus: Woman, Photographer, Godmother," "Symbolism from a Feminist Perspective," and "Victorian Press and the Female Body." Interviews have featured an interesting variety of women: a feminist sculptor, a feminist psychotherapist, Gloria Steinem, May Sarton, others.

Some publications in this category are primarily regional, although available by subscription. Among the most familiar is *Sojourner* (443 Albany St., Cambridge, MA 02139), a monthly New England women's journal "of news, opinion, and the arts," published as a newspaper of twenty or more pages. *Sojourner* encourages readers to submit reviews, feature articles, brief items of women's news, fiction, and poetry. Reviews are especially numerous and wide-ranging—books on literature, history, psychology, health, and politics are considered, as well as fiction and poetry, and theater, films, visual arts, and music are also reviewed. Viewpoint topics have ranged from "Anti-Semitism and the Women's Movement" to "Art Education: Coloring by Gender." And *Sojourner* prints long and thoughtful letters from readers.

From Washington, D.C., comes *Off Our Backs*, a monthly "women's news journal" also in newspaper form (1724 20th St., N.W., Washington, DC 20008). Edited by a collective, this journal "welcomes" unsolicited contributions: "We publish news (health, prison, gay, international, labor, legal), reviews (music, books, art), poetry, survival, and commentaries." A recent issue included "Women in Botswana: Oppressed Lives," by a recent Ph.D. in South African politics, a report entitled "Feminist Theories of Science," lengthy speculative book reviews, dozens of news items, and letters. *Off Our Backs* seems to share space generously among a wide variety of contributors. *Heliotrope* (bimonthly; 2755 Macomb St., Washington, DC 20008), an eight-page newsletter, prints long book reviews, profiles, and essays on personal experience. One issue featured an interview-profile of Tillie Olsen. *Spokeswoman* (Mary Blake French, ed; 854 National Press Building, Washington, DC 20045), a feminist-produced national news magazine, publishes news summaries of the women's movement, including the arts. Recent articles have studied Judy Chicago and the implications of the Bakke decision. Unsolicited reviews (often quite brief) of fiction, women's diaries, scholarly works, feminist fiction for children, and films are considered.

New Directions for Women, a quarterly feminist newspaper (223 Old Hook Rd., Westwood, NJ 07675), prints short articles on subjects of special interest to feminists, such as the future of women's studies, evolving theories of feminism, women in dance, theater, sports. Reviews are numerous and varied: one issue evaluated, among other books, poems by Susan Griffin, fiction by Charlotte Perkins Gilman, literary criticism about Edith Wharton, Virginia Woolf, and women in American literature. A section of brief women's news items solicits reports on local "conferences, women's groups, consciousness-raising, politics, etcetera" from readers across the country. *Motherroot* (c/o Anne Pride, Motherroot Publications, 214 Dewey St., Pittsburgh, PA

15218), also a quarterly in newspaper form, is a new "women's review of small presses" that concentrates on books "by women, of special interest to women and/or about women" that may not get the critical attention they deserve elsewhere. Some of the books reviewed are published and distributed by their authors (Jeannie G. Pool, *Women in Music History*); others come from feminist presses (*Calamity Jane's Letter to Her Daughter,* Shameless Hussy) or university presses (Sara Royce's *A Frontier Lady,* Univ. of Nebraska). Only books from "presses which have a good reputation concerning women's issues" are considered. In its first issue, *Motherroot* requested contributions of reviews and of "essays about women's literature and culture."

A special-interest publication is *Feminary: A Feminist Journal for the South, Emphasizing the Lesbian Vision* (Box 954, Chapel Hill, NC 27514). *Feminary*'s recent call for articles requested:

news and events of local lesbian communities; theoretical and practical articles; short prose and poetry; feminist scholarship; criticism and essays on the Southern experience from a radical perspective, in a non-academic style, reclaiming our past; humor, drawings, and photographs. [Editors also] encourage women who are not lesbians but are working on these materials to submit materials.

Beyond the world of specifically feminist publications, newspapers offer a rich array of publishing possibilities. A good place to start is the op-ed essay. Many large papers open the page adjoining the editorials to opinion pieces by free-lancers, and some pay for contributions. Subjects can range from the personal—as in Linda Bird Francke's now well-known *New York Times* piece on her abortion—to the general issues affecting women—the ERA, sexist language, implications of the Bakke decision. Among the major papers that pay for op-ed pieces are the *New York Times* (229 W. 43rd St., New York, NY 10036; $150 maximum), the *Chicago Sun Times* (401 N.Wabash Ave., Chicago, IL 60611; $35 minimum), *Newsday* (550 Stewart Ave., Garden City, NY 11550; $50-$500), and the *Los Angeles Times* (Times Mirror Square, Los Angeles, CA 90053). The length of op-ed essays may vary from 500 to 2,000 words, but 700 words is most usual. Also worth a try is *Newsweek Magazine*'s "My Turn" page (444 Madison Ave., New York, NY 10022), which accepts unsolicited manuscripts of up to 1,100 words and has printed essays on a wide range of topics, weighty and humorous, by known and unknown writers (most of them, recently, male).

Sunday newspaper magazines offer two possibilities. One is the short excerpt from research in progress, rewritten for general readers. Nothing expands the value of academic research more than getting it out to the wide readership of a Sunday newspaper. If your master's thesis is "Women and the British Occupation of Boston," the *Boston*

Globe's magazine might buy your idea. Or a Cincinnati Sunday magazine might be receptive to an article on the many women potters (at Rookwood and in independent studios) who clustered in that city during the last quarter of the nineteenth century.

Sunday magazines also run profiles. Biographers can and do publish shorter articles on women who have been "lost" or "hidden from history," especially locally. For example, in 1979 the *New York Times Magazine,* in addition to articles about well-known women like Toni Morrison and Joan Didion, ran a long profile (by a man) of May Edward Chinn, a practicing eighty-three-year-old Harlem physician and musician. The reminiscences of family or older friends may provide clues about such a woman, dead or living, as may a public building, school, or library named after a woman, and a trip to the local historical society or library may turn up journals, letters, or a privately printed family history. Women writers are sometimes ignored in the places where they spent their lives. A recent Sunday feature in a St. Louis paper, for example, surveyed the connections of dozens of writers to that city, but never mentioned Kate Chopin, who was born, lived, died, and wrote for nearly forty years in St. Louis and whose earliest fiction dealt with local history. Certainly St. Louis readers are due for a feature on Chopin—or perhaps Marianne Moore, also born there. Willa Cather's Virginia birthplace, about which she wrote her last novel, *Sapphira and the Slave Girl,* still stands, largely unobserved by locals, another likely starting point for a newspaper feature (Winchester is the nearest city).

Even a small local newspaper may provide a starting place for presenting women's issues to a wide range of nonacademic readers. For instance, a weekly newspaper in a small midwestern town has recently published several interesting features by a local woman. One, begun by a visit to the local graveyard, considered effects of infant mortality on nineteenth-century local women. Another, a pungent piece of oral feminist history, developed from interviews with a woman who has clerked in the town drugstore for the past thirty-five years.

A woman writer on the lecture circuit or in residence at a nearby school can offer an even more timely approach to getting published in daily or Sunday newspapers. Readings usually include a question-and-answer session. You may also find the writer herself, or a publicity-eager university department, willing to cooperate in scheduling a private interview, especially if you have sold the story idea in advance, to ensure that the article will get into print while the appearance is still news. This is a field in which well-informed critics still sometimes seem to be in short supply. For instance, a recent university fiction symposium included five well-known novelists, four of them male. Dialogues among the four men, edited and introduced by a local professor, were published in two large-circulation national magazines. The woman's comments were reported only in a campus newspaper. Certainly a missed opportunity for a feminist critic!

Letters to the editor are often overlooked as a means to get started as a published writer. They are, to be sure, frequently too short and perfunctory to be read seriously, but some publications do print short essays in response to articles. Michele Murray, the late critic and poet, got her start as a reviewer by writing a lengthy response to a *Commonweal* article on the role of the educated mother. The magazine ran her entire letter, and she soon had an offer to write free-lance reviews for a similar publication.

Most book reviews in newspapers or magazines are either written by staff or assigned to free-lancers. But a response to a review can inject feminist criticism and consciousness raising in a forum where your words may influence many book buyers and can be especially useful when a feminist book has been misunderstood by the reviewer. Or conversely, when a writer who claims to be a feminist writes an antiwoman book, an incisive letter hits the mark. Both the *New York Review of Books* (250 W. 57th St., New York, NY 10019) and the Sunday *New York Times Book Review* frequently run long responses from readers, as may local newspapers.

Another large possible outlet for feminist writers is the commercial magazines, or the "slicks," as Sylvia Plath called some of them. Plath's own diligent attack on these magazines is inspiring and exhausting: she tried to have "out" as many as twenty manuscripts of poems, fiction, and nonfiction, aimed at such diverse targets as *Seventeen, Atlantic Monthly, Mademoiselle, Ladies' Home Journal, Art News,* and *Woman's Day.* Acceptances (and rejections) began to accrue while she was still in high school. Today, the best reason for writing for such publications is the large circulation they guarantee. As Charlotte Bunch says in her article on feminist journals elsewhere in this volume, the major drawback to publishing with the feminist presses is their limited circulation, even though such journals do get passed around and shared. Also, commercial magazines pay for articles, from modest fees to big ones, so there are obvious advantages to sending one's work to them as well as to academic and feminist publications.

Beginning with magazines aimed primarily at women, one thinks first of the success story of feminist publications, *Ms. Magazine* (119 W. 40th St., New York, NY 10018), which began as a commercial monthly and is now published by Ms. Foundation for Education and Communication. *Ms.* elicits a variety of responses from feminist writers, some of whom have had trouble getting material accepted and disagreements over editorial changes made in their manuscripts. Lacking personal experience with *Ms.*, we suggest that new contributors send short pieces to a regular feature called *Ms. Gazette.* According to *Writer's Market,* "it is possible to move from the Gazette to do other work for *Ms.*" The feature usually appears in two sections. One, News from All Over, collects brief, sometimes signed accounts of feminist events, activities, and media coverage and an occasional historical item. Subjects have included exhibits of women's art, new publications, court decisions, women's participation in the Civil War, and a short account of the rediscovery of an early American feminist by a woman who is writing a book on her. According to editors, *Ms.* "would like more input on what women are doing in their communities" for this department. The second section of the Gazette devotes several pages to a single issue; it is usually written by a single author (often a free-lancer or an academic). Subjects have included a survey of new feminist periodicals, a bibliography of feminist books for children, and "A Sampling of New Finds in Women's Studies" (a group of brief reviews). Articles in *Ms.* proper cover a variety of subjects and have included some important literary essays—on Charlotte Brontë, Zora Neale Hurston, Iris Murdoch, and others. *Ms.* on the Arts publishes reviews of books, art, music, and films, and the magazine's fiction and poetry pages, while sprinkled with familiar names (Rich, Walker, Atwood), have also included a previously unpublished classmate of ours.

Other women's magazines that are not apparently feminist have changed considerably since the 1950s, despite a feminist undergraduate's recent complaint that "all they ever talk about is staying home, cooking and sewing, crocheting doilies and making quilts" (quoted in Joyce Maynard, "Hers," *New York Times,* 29 March 1979, p. C2). *Vogue* (250 Madison Ave., New York, NY 10017) and *Mademoiselle* (same address) have always published some work of literary merit, and they continue to do so. Every *Mademoiselle* includes fiction, and feature articles have covered such subjects as writing careers for women and "Why Do Men Suddenly Want to Be Fathers? Especially When A Lot of Women Don't Want to Be Mothers?" as well as reports on the National Women's Conference, a National Conference on Men and Masculinity, and Judy Chicago's recent work. *Mademoiselle* pays $100 and up for an article of 1,800-6,000 words. Writers of nonfiction should send a query, along with samples of published or unpublished work. Another fashion magazine, *Glamour* (350 Madison Ave., New York, NY 10017), invites reader contributions to a monthly Viewpoint column: "Do you have a cause you'd like to support? Or a grievance to air?" Contributors receive $300 for manuscripts of 1,000-1,200 words. In a recent Viewpoint column, a writing teacher discussed the decline of our "language of feeling."

Even such doggedly domestic standbys as *Ladies Home Journal* (641 Lexington Ave., New York, NY 10020), *McCalls* (230 Park Ave., New

York, NY 10017), *Redbook* (same address), *Woman's Day* (1515 Broadway, New York, NY 10017), and *Family Circle* (488 Madison Ave., New York, NY 10022) now reflect the expanding interests of their readers. Most have departments similar to *Ms.* Gazette that would be likely targets for brief items of news or history. Feature articles may touch on such issues as child care, occupational reentry, and obstetric and gynecological health—for example, a recent *Redbook* report "The New Wisdom about Menstruation." *Redbook* has also published "How to Get Hired for More Money," "God and Woman" (by a free-lancer who is a student of comparative religions), and a reflective analysis, "Four Waitresses: Their Secret World." A monthly *Redbook* column of personal experience, "A Young Mother's Story," solicits contributions of 1,000-2,000 words from readers and pays $500. A typical piece might recount the reaction of a feminist teacher to sexism encountered by her daughter in elementary school or the experiences of a college student who has been a welfare mother ("How I Beat the Welfare Trap"). In *Writer's Market, Redbook's* editor suggests that the best way to break into the magazine is through its varied and generous fiction pages, which have included stories by Toni Cade Bambara, Rosellen Brown, Anne Tyler, and Carson McCullers. Several well-known writers of fiction published their first stories in *Redbook*.

The prestigious literary and opinion magazines—*Atlantic Monthly* (8 Arlington St., Boston, MA 02116), *New Republic* (1220 19th St., N.W., Washington, DC 20036), *Nation* (72 Fifth Ave., New York, NY 10011), *Saturday Review* (1290 Ave. of the Americas, New York, NY 10022), *Commentary* (165 E. 56th St., New York, NY 10036)—obviously are, or at least should be, receptive to short studies of women or to feminist book reviews. Reviews of books by and about women do appear regularly in all, but a survey of recent issues turns up a depressingly small number of articles by and about women. Features such as Shelia Tobias' "Who's Afraid of Math, and Why" in *Atlantic Monthly* are all too few. *Commentary* and *New Republic* (half of which is written by free-lancers) seem more receptive than most to women's topics, and the *Nation* appears eager for new contributors. Its editor says, "we welcome all articles dealing with the social scene, particularly if they examine it with a new point of view or expose conditions the rest of the media overlook." The *Nation* is looking for non–New York contributors, in places "where we don't have anyone." And, as *Writer's Market* suggests, new publications may be particularly open to new contributors, especially in their book review sections. Two possibilities are *Mother Jones* (607 Market St., San Francisco, CA 94105) and *Quest 79* (1133 Ave. of the Americas, New York, NY 10036). *Quest 79* recently published Peter F. Drucker's portrait of his grandmother and an article about the relationship of a Mexican-American woman and her daughter at Yale. For these and all other commercial publications, check *Writer's Market* for details of subject matter, length, payment, and manuscript submission.

Finally, feminist writers might consider a large mixed bag of special-interest publications. Some are primarily regional. Virtually every large American city now has its own magazine, publishing notes on current events, reviews of city attractions, and investigative articles on local life. *Cincinnati Magazine* has recently published a woman writer's exposé of a sexist children's television program that has been a local institution for years, an investigative survey of women's organizations within the city, and a review of a mother-daughter-granddaughter show at a local art gallery. *San Francisco* published an illustrated review article on photographer Imogen Cunningham—and your local magazine is sure to provide similar possibilities. Other regional publications vary widely in type. *Yankee* (Dublin, NH 03444), among recipes and homey anecdotes of New England culture, has published reports on women's businesses and a recent critical profile of poet Maxine Kumin. *Missouri Life* (bimonthly; 1209 Elmerine Ave., Jefferson City, MO 65101), a glossily attractive (if determinedly non-controversial) magazine, solicits articles covering "history, travel, recreation, human interest, personality, profiles, business, scenic, folklore"—suggesting many possibilities for women writers. *Mountain Life and Work*, a monthly tabloid, calls itself "The Magazine of the Appalachian South" and welcomes manuscripts (Council of the Southern Mountains, Inc., Drawer N, Clintwood, VA 24228). Articles are usually brief and concentrate largely on issues of work, especially in the mines—for example, "Coal Mining and Women." Reviews consider regional publications: fiction, reprints, others. *Ohioana Quarterly* (1105 Ohio Department Building, 65 S. Front St., Columbus, OH 43215) consists entirely of articles on Ohio writers (e.g., Toni Morrison) and reviews of their work. Your own region almost certainly has similar publications.

Other special interest publications emphasize American history. Probably the best known of these is *American Heritage* (bimonthly; 10 Rockefeller Plaza, New York, NY 10020). A recent feature, "Years Came Along One after the Other," is an excerpt from a group of memoirs by Kansas pioneer women, collected by a woman early in this century and now being edited by her great-granddaughter, a university student. "She Couldn't Have Done It, Even If She Did" is a woman's reconsideration of Lizzie Borden, and "Selling the Swedish Nightingale" examines the economic relationship of Jenny Lind and P. T. Barnum. A regular department, American Characters, occasionally profiles women from American history, such as Aimee Semple McPherson. And another feature, Reader's Album, pays $50 to readers for publishing "unusual, dramatic, or 'what's going on here?' photographs that they own." This section might provide an opportunity for presenting photographs unearthed in women's studies research to a large audience. Another handsome historical publication, also aimed at general readers, is *American West: The Magazine of Western History* (Suite 160, 20380 Town Center Lane, Cupertino, CA 95014). Features have included oral history from a Texas frontier woman, edited by a free-lancer, and "Jessie Benton Fremont: The Story of a Remarkable Nineteenth-Century Woman"; reviews are also published. *Americana* (10 Rockefeller Plaza, New York, NY 10020) publishes relatively brief articles on the material culture of America's past. For example, "Bedspreads from the Blue Mountains" considers an early women's industry; "Quilts of Baltimore" recounts research that at last identified two celebrated American quiltmakers.

A last group of special-interest publications comes from institutions. Some are published by museums; thick, glossy *Smithsonian* (monthly; 900 Jefferson Dr., Washington, DC 20560), for example, includes articles on art, current events, and natural and cultural history, as well as reviews. Recent issues included Miriam Troop's article on two little-known colonial American painters who were women, John J. Tarrant's "The Woman Who Inspired American Impressionism," and Ann Hoskell's evocation of a medieval woman's life. Other periodicals, published by state historical societies, should be receptive to articles on women connected to their areas. *Bulletin of the Missouri Historical Society* published Per Seyersted's first article on Kate Chopin; *Louisiana History* published Marie Fletcher's "The Southern Woman in the Fiction of Kate Chopin." Local historical societies may have their own publications: *Cincinnati Historical Society Bulletin,* for example, recently included an article on local lectures by Frances Wright, in her time "the most eloquent voice in America for change and social justice." Libraries, too, sponsor promising publications, such as *Wilson Library Bulletin,* a substantial journal, or the *Newberry Newsletter.* For example, *Colby Library Quarterly* (Waterville, ME 04901), a small literary journal, specializes in articles (under 20 pages) on Maine writers (including Sarah Orne Jewett and Edna Millay) and on writers represented in the library's special collections or having influence on Maine literature (such as Willa Cather and Ellen Glasgow).

In this article we have only scratched the surface of publication possibilities for women's studies scholars. Every day we encounter new and additional possibilities—as do you. So, when the question "But how do I get published?" arises in your life, don't conclude that the answer must be *Signs* or nothing. Consider the newsletters that cram your mailbox—or your neighbor's—at home and at work, the newspapers on your doorstep, the magazines on your table, in your dentist's office, in your friend's fist. An exploratory stroll through the current periodicals reading room of your library will turn up dozens of publications that might welcome a contribution from you—as will a long look at the corner newsstand. Even the airline flight magazine in the pocket at your knees accepts lively free-lance articles on current issues. It should now be clear that getting published need not be a formidable, overwhelming obstacle. All you need is a copy of *Writer's Market* under your arm, a willingness to start small, some imagination about subjects and formats, an open mind—and we'll soon be reading you.

Notes on Contributors

Angelika Bammer has taught community college, continuing education, and university courses in women's studies and modern languages. She began her academic studies at the University of Heidelberg and is completing her Ph.D. in comparative literature at the University of Wisconsin, Madison, with a dissertation on the utopian impulse in feminist fictions.

Charlotte Bunch, a feminist writer, activist, speaker, and editor, was one of the founders of Women's Liberation in Washington, D.C., in 1968. She has edited six feminist anthologies, including *Building Feminist Theory: Essays from* Quest, based on the first years of *Quest: A Feminist Quarterly*, of which she was a founding editor. She is currently working on issues of global feminism with Interfem Consultants in New York.

Ralph Carlson is Vice-President at Garland Publishing, a firm specializing in scholarly reprints and in original reference books. Before coming to Garland he was Senior Editor at Northwestern University Press. He says he had the good sense never to finish a Ph.D. in philosophy.

Shirley Frank, a graduate of Barnard College, holds a Ph.D. in English and American literature from Brandeis University. She has taught English and women's studies, and is currently Managing Editor of *Women's Studies Quarterly*, a copublication of the Feminist Press and the National Women's Studies Association.

Susan Griffin, who makes her living writing and teaching in the Bay area, is a poet, essayist, and philosopher.

Joan E. Hartman was a member and cochair of the MLA Commission on the Status of Women in the Profession. She is Professor of English and Chairperson of the department at the College of Staten Island, City University of New York.

Martha M. Kinney has worked in academic and trade book publishing since 1970 and is now Senior Editor at Viking-Penguin, Inc. She comes from Oklahoma.

Ronald Mallis is Vice-President for development at Education for Management, Inc. He previously worked in publishing for a dozen years as both a manuscript and an acquisitions editor; when he wrote his essay, he was English editor of Houghton Mifflin Company.

Ellen Messer-Davidow was a member of the MLA Commission on the Status of Women in the Profession, a founder and coordinator of the MLA Graduate Student Caucus, and Administrative Assistant to the President of the University of Cincinnati. She is currently completing a doctoral dissertation on feminist critical theory.

Carol Orr, formerly Assistant Director of Princeton University Press, is Director of the University of Tennessee Press. A member of the board of directors of the Association of American University Presses, she is past president of Women in Scholarly Publishing (WISP).

Jean A. Perkins is Susan Lippincott Professor of French literature at Swarthmore College. She has published *The Concept of Self in the French Enlightenment* with Droz of Paris as well as articles in various journals, including *Studies on Voltaire and the Eighteenth Century,* also produced abroad. She has been member and cochair of the MLA Commission on the Status of Women in the Profession and president of the Modern Language Association.

Ann Romines received her Ph.D. in American literature from George Washington University with a dissertation on the uses of domestic ritual in American women's fiction. She has taught American and women's literature at the University of Cincinnati and is now at George Washington University. She has recently published essays on Sarah Orne Jewett and Eudora Welty.

Thomazine W. Shanahan, who earned a master's degree in women's studies from George Washington University, is a Washington, D.C., free-lance writer. Her work has been published in newspapers and academic journals.

Domna C. Stanton, a former member and cochair of the MLA Commission on the Status of Women in the Profession, is Professor of French and Women's Studies at the University of Michigan. The author of *The Aristocrat as Art* and a forthcoming anthology of French feminist poetry, she has also published articles on feminist literary criticism and seventeenth-century French literature. She was the Associate Editor of *Signs* from 1974 to 1980, and she still serves on the journal's editorial board.

Emily Toth, an Assistant Professor of English at Pennsylvania State University, is coauthor of *The Curse: A Cultural History of Menstruation* and assistant editor of *A Kate Chopin Miscellany.* Her most recent book is *Inside Peyton Place: The Life of Grace Metalious.* She edited *Regionalism and the Female Imagination* (formerly the *Kate Chopin Newsletter*) from 1975 to 1979, when it ceased publication.

J. J. Wilson, Professor of English at Sonoma State University, works chiefly on Virginia Woolf, women's issues, and interdisciplinary studies.